Writing As Liberation

BY

NICOLE YARDE

Dedication

To the radiant memory of my grandmother, Edna Louise Harding—you were the heartbeat of my stories, the warmth that fueled my dreams, and the forever light that guided me through every chapter of life. Your love was a compass, your faith my strength, and every word I've written carries the imprint of the stories you first shared with me.

To my incredible family and my cherished girlfriends—you have been my sanctuary and my constant source of strength. In moments of laughter and in times of tears, you've stood by me, offering boundless support, loving honesty, and endless inspiration. Thank you for the late-night heart-to-hearts, the early-morning encouragements, and for always knowing when it was time for a comforting cup of coffee or a glass of wine. Your belief in me carried me through my darkest days, and your love is a foundation I will forever cherish.

To my rock, my applesauce and my partner in every sense—your quiet encouragement was the gentle force I needed to move forward. You believed in my words even when I doubted them. Your wisdom, patience, and unshakable support lifted me closer to the future I didn't always see for myself. There are no words vast enough to express the depth of my gratitude and my love I have for you.

This book is a reflection of every soul who touched my journey with grace, love, and encouragement. I carry each of you in my heart, and this is as much of your story as it is mine.

And finally, to you, the reader—thank you for allowing me the privilege of your time, your attention, and your heart. It is my deepest hope that within these pages, you find a spark of inspiration that propels you toward your own Liberation. May this journey we've shared remind you that your voice, your story, and your dreams are all worthy of the light.

With endless gratitude,

Nicole Yarde

Contents

> *Embarking on a transformative journey of self-discovery and liberation through writing.*

My Journey: From "Just Words" to Liberation

Writing was never *just* something I did—it was my lifeline. Growing up in a middle-class Caribbean household, raised by an old-school grandmother, we had a few outlets for speaking our minds freely. I was raised under the doctrine that children were seen, not heard, so if you had a problem, you either solved it with food, prayer, or hard work. Therapy wasn't an option. In fact, it wasn't even a word that was in our vocabulary (if you know, you know). So, writing became my silent refuge long before I understood what healing really was. When life felt like too much—when the noise of the world threatened to drown me out—I found sanctuary in my journals. Those pages were where I poured out the questions I couldn't ask, the fears I couldn't speak, and the hopes I kept close to my chest. Writing, for some, may have been regulated to just school assignments; for me, it was how I stayed tethered to myself in a world that often felt overwhelming or didn't feel like it was made for me.

As I grew, so did my relationship with writing. It evolved from a private escape into a craft, something I proudly honed. I earned degrees in Journalism and English, then a Master's in International Education, and with each step, I built a body of work that carried my truth, my stories, and the stories of those around me. Writing became my quiet strength—when my dialect marked me as an outsider, my writing brought me in, allowing me to speak in spaces where I might have otherwise been silent.

And then, one day, that strength was tested.

A few years ago, while working in a corporate-ish job, I was tasked with writing a critical fundraising document. I'd done this type of work many times before, successfully I might add, but this particular assignment felt more personal. The funds were for students in historically neglected communities—communities that reflected my own experiences and those of some people I knew. I poured my heart and soul into it, writing with a profound sense of purpose, acutely aware of the impact these funds could have.

The day was here that I had to submit my assignment. I took the initiative not to wait for when the assignment was requested, and I got the attention of my supervisor (it was very much the adult version of "teacher, teacher, look, I finished my homework"). I anxiously handed my document to my supervisor, someone I admired and respected. I felt a sense of pride in what I had written, knowing it mattered. But after glancing at it for what felt like all of 10.58 seconds, the person flippantly handed it back to me with a shrug and said, and I quote, "These are just words."

Just words.

Those two words landed like a punch to the gut, and as those words hit my psyche, so did my ass hit the chair. I felt like a child being sent to time out—small, unimportant, unseen. I sat back, trying to swallow the sting of the comment, trying not to let the disappointment show – and the Aquarius in me wasn't about to show any sign of weakness. But deep down, those words left a mark. They sent me into a spiral of doubt, questioning my worth, abilities, and the very thing that had always been my sanctuary: my writing.

You might be wondering *why did I let that one comment shake me so much*. Girl, brush that off and keep it moving, and usually I do, but this one hit differently because writing was never "just" anything to me.

Writing was my secret superpower, the quiet strength that had carried me through some of the loneliest times when I felt unseen, unheard, and misunderstood. My words helped me earn thousands of dollars in college scholarships for young brown and Black students, got me through college, aided me throughout my career, and allowed me to be in spaces that were historically not built for me. My writing was both personal and communal, a way for me to connect with myself, give back to others, and give voice to those who had none. When my supervisor casually reduced it all to *just words*, it felt like a part of me had been stripped away.

Please don't misunderstand—I'm not someone who runs from criticism, nor am I that fragile. Growing up as the only girl in a house full of boys, I learned very quickly how to develop a thick skin and a quick wit. I fully embrace constructive criticism as a tool for growth. But this wasn't about constructive feedback. This felt like a dismissal, a rejection of something that had always given me strength.

I sat there in my cubicle, earbuds in, grappling with what had transpired. The sting of the comment was undeniable, but it was the sudden wave of insecurity that genuinely shocked me. In the days that followed, I found myself unraveling. Doubt crept in like an unwanted guest, questioning everything I thought I knew about myself. *Am I really a good writer? Do my words even matter? Had I been fooling myself all this time?* For weeks, I obsessed over every word I wrote. I re-read emails, second-guessed drafts, and hesitated to share my work. That tiny seed of doubt had blossomed into a suffocating forest within me, and the longer I allowed it to take root, the smaller I felt.

Maybe you've been there, too, where you've had moments where someone's offhand remark left you doubting yourself, your talent, and your dreams. Maybe, like me, you've questioned whether your voice really matters.

But then, something happened.

A sharp, direct, and unrelentingly honest friend asked me a question that jolted me out of the fog: *"When did you decide to give away your power?"* Granted, he said a bit more than that, but I will spare you the profanity; just know what he said worked.

It was the stern wake-your-ass-up-reclaim-your-strength call that I needed. At that moment, I realized that it wasn't just my supervisor's comment that had broken me—it was the power I had allowed it to have over me. I had surrendered my voice, my sense of worth, without even realizing it. I had let someone else's perception silence me, and in doing so, I had silenced myself.

That realization was the turning point. I knew I had to reclaim the power I had so easily and quickly given away. I had to reclaim my voice.

I began asking myself uncomfortable but necessary questions: *Who am I when I stop trying to live up to someone else's idea of me? Why did those words cut so deeply? Can I trust myself to be vulnerable again? Why do you write in the first place?*

The answers came slowly; day by day, with every word I wrote, I began to find my strength again. I reconnected to my truth: my words were never just words. They were pieces of my soul; they held power and carried significance. And so do yours. If you're reading this, I know you've had moments like this too. Moments where doubt crept in and tried to make you believe that your story, your voice, didn't matter.

As you move through these pages, I hope you come to understand the significance of your voice in a deeper, more powerful way, recognizing your story as a source of strength rather than something to be questioned. Your words carry the essence of who you are—they are not "just words" but your truth. In them, you will find the freedom you've been searching for. This book is about reclaiming that power, confronting the doubts, critics, and fears that have held you back, and stepping fully into your strength. It is a journey of self-discovery, finding freedom through writing, and ultimately using your words to create the life you've always dreamed of.

I'm sharing this journey with you because I believe in the power of words to heal, to inspire, and to transform. Writing has been my way of making sense of the world, and now, I'm inviting you to do the same.

Freedom Dreaming: Turning Words into Action

Imagine a world where your deepest desires for freedom and justice become reality. This is the power of freedom dreaming, the radical act of envisioning a future unbound by the chains of oppression. On my path to self-discovery, I came across a book that forever changed the way I saw the world and myself—*Freedom Dreams: The Black Radical Imagination* by Robin D.G. Kelley. It felt like a mirror, reflecting the hopes and desires I had carried for so long but had never fully articulated. Kelley's idea of freedom dreaming spoke to something deep within me, something I had felt but never fully expressed. It introduced me to the power of collective vision, of daring to dream of a world free from injustice.

Kelley speaks of collective liberation, movements that shake the foundations of injustice. While his focus is on societal transformation, the lessons in *Freedom Dreams* resonate just as deeply on a personal level. Writing became the gateway to my own liberation. It became how I translated those radical dreams into something tangible and real.

That's the heart of Not Just Words (thank you, Kelley). Here, we take Kelley's concept and bring it home to the most personal space: your own life. Through journaling, storytelling, and creative practice, you can create the life you've always known you were meant to live. Each word you write becomes an act of reclamation, a path toward radical self-expression and true freedom.

And it all starts with a choice: the courage to imagine something different.

What is freedom dreaming? It is the act of envisioning a life that rises above the constraints imposed by society, culture, or even your own doubts. It's the moment when you allow yourself to stand on the edge of possibility and let go of the expectations that have weighed you down. Picture yourself living without fear, without the pressure to meet someone else's idea of who you should be. What does your world look like when you are fully free to create it?

Once you allow yourself to dream freely, the next step is finding the courage to bring those visions to life. Kelley's words have stayed with me: "Without new visions, we don't know what to build, only what to knock down." This journal is here to help you build that vision, to turn your dreams into something tangible. It invites you to ask more profound questions: Am I living the life I want? And if the answer is no, what steps can I take to begin shaping the future I deserve?

Reflect for a moment: What belief is holding me back? Take a deep breath and write down one action you can take today to challenge that belief. Your dreams are not distant fantasies; they are the first step toward change.

At the heart of freedom dreaming is the understanding that envisioning a better world is an active, not passive, process. For writers, this means using creativity to transcend the limitations of the present moment. When you write, each word and sentence is an act of defiance. You are daring to imagine a world that doesn't yet exist but could be—a world where justice, equality, and freedom are the foundation of everything we create.

Even though this book takes an intimate, personal look into writing, I would be remiss to ignore that we start with you, the individual, but we can't ignore the power of collective dreaming, which is undeniable. When writers—especially those from marginalized communities—join forces, their collective vision creates a greater momentum than any one person's voice. This is how liberation stops being a distant dream and starts becoming a reality. By amplifying each other's visions, we weave together stories that become impossible to ignore. The words of Audre Lorde, James Baldwin, and Toni Morrison weren't just personal expressions; they became part of a global call for justice and change. Their stories lit a path for others to follow, proving that our individual voices are never isolated. When we write, when we dream together, we shape a movement.

So, when you write, remember you are contributing to a legacy of visionaries who believed in the power of words to create change. Your words joined with others, become part of a chorus demanding justice, calling for equality, and refusing to be silenced.

Freedom dreaming asks something of you: to write for the future you are determined to create. Your imagination is a force that can reshape reality and build bridges between what is and what could be. Your words can shift minds, inspire action, and help create a world where freedom is not a distant ideal but a lived experience.

The more you engage with this process, the more expansive it becomes. Every time you put pen to paper or fingers to keyboard, you participate in the act of creation. You are building the future you once only dreamed of. And when you share that vision with others, something even more powerful happens. Collective dreaming takes root. Writers from every corner of the world, especially those who have been silenced, join their voices in creating a world where freedom is not an aspiration but a reality.

This is how change happens: through the voices of those who dare to dream, who refuse to wait for permission. It begins with you. Your imagination, your words—they hold the key. So, what is your vision for the future? How will you use your words to build it?

The Transformative Power of Freedom Dreaming for Writers

Let's acknowledge the truth: this journey will be challenging. It's not a passive activity where enlightenment arrives effortlessly. This work demands staunch dedication and an unwavering commitment to your authentic self. The path to liberation isn't a leisurely stroll; it's a demanding ascent, often steep and challenging. But with each step you take, with every word you commit to paper, you inch closer to the life you yearn to create. You possess a wellspring of strength within, and this journal will serve as your guide to uncovering it.

Remember, you're not here to conform to someone else's expectations or adhere to pre-determined rules. You're here to construct your own path, to nurture your dreams, and to liberate yourself through the act of writing. Every sentence you craft, every story you unveil, is a bold reclamation of your inherent power. This journey is about discovering your unique voice, forging your own path, and defiantly refusing to be silenced.

As you navigate these pages, anticipate a profound transformation. You'll be encouraged to delve into the depths of your being, to venture beyond the confines of your comfort zone, and to embrace dreams more expansive than you ever thought possible. You'll find inspiration in the carefully curated quotes, grounded in empowering affirmations, and a spark of creativity ignited by the thoughtfully designed exercises, all intended to reconnect you with your inner power.

You're human, navigating a human experience with feelings that are completely normal—dare I say, human. Inevitably, there will be moments of doubt. Take a breath; it's okay. There will be days when the act of writing feels laborious, and the temptation to surrender looms large. But these moments are not indicative of failure; they are integral to the process. Freedom dreaming necessitates persistence, an unwavering, determined march forward, regardless of the pace. Each challenge you encounter is an opportunity to cultivate resilience and fortify the foundations of the life you deserve.

This journal exists for a profound purpose: to empower you to reclaim your voice, to serve as a steadfast companion as you write your way to freedom, and to midwife the stories within you that yearn to be expressed. Time is of the essence. The longer you delay, the fainter your voice becomes, and the stakes couldn't be higher. If you hesitate, those stories, brimming with unique insights and perspectives, may remain forever concealed. The world eagerly awaits the brilliance that only you can offer.

Therefore, seize your pen and begin writing your future into existence with steadfast determination.

And to my former supervisor, I extend my gratitude. What you once dismissed as "just words" has blossomed into the very essence of my purpose.

Welcome to the Beginning of Your Liberation Journey

Hey there, Dreamer of Freedom!

Welcome to *Not Just Words: Writing as Liberation*—your own personal guide to breaking free and finding your voice. Think of it as a treasure map, leading you through four exciting landmarks: Self-Discovery, Voice Empowerment, Confronting Barriers, and Manifesting Your Reality. By the end of this journey, you'll know yourself better, understand the power of your unique voice, and know how to blast through any obstacle in your way. And the best part? You'll learn how to turn those fantastic dreams into something real. Each chapter is like a stepping stone, bringing you closer to the truly free you.

All I ask is that you embrace vulnerability as you write, for it is in the depths of our authentic selves that we discover true freedom. Dive deep, be honest, and let your true self shine through—that's where the magic happens. Let your curiosity be your compass and your passions your fuel as you navigate the pages of this journal. Whether you're yearning to reclaim your voice, reignite your creative spark, or shatter the barriers holding you back, *Not Just Words: Writing as Liberation* is your trusty sidekick on this awesome adventure of self-discovery.

As you embrace this process, you'll begin to understand that liberation and freedom are not just ideals—they are lived experiences ready to be claimed. Liberation is the exhilarating climb, the persistent struggle to break free from the chains that bind you. Freedom is the summit, the breathtaking view of a life lived on your own terms, without limitations. With this journal as your guide, you'll experience both. You'll move from breaking through those walls to breaking free and taking flight. So, grab your pen, and let's get started! Your voice, your story, your liberation—it's all waiting for you.

Here's what you can expect on this journey:

▶ **Stage 1: Self-Discovery** (Chapters 1-3)

You'll start by revealing the various layers of your identity. Who are you beyond the labels and roles society has given you? You'll dive deep into understanding the stories you tell yourself and begin unearthing the real you. This is where you'll reclaim your narrative and realize that your words are more than just words—they're your truth.

▶ **Stage 2: Overcoming Inner Barriers** (Chapters 4-6)

Every creative journey has roadblocks, and in this stage, you'll confront the inner critic, the doubt, and the fears that have kept you from writing freely. You'll learn to silence those negative voices and replace them with affirmations that empower your writing. By the end of this stage, your confidence will have grown, and you'll be ready to express yourself fully.

▶ **Stage 3: Crafting Your Authentic Voice** (Chapters 7-9)

Once you've silenced the inner critic, you'll start honing your authentic voice. You'll explore your heritage, personal stories, and unique perspective, crafting writing that resonates deeply with you and your readers. This stage is about unlocking the full power of your voice so that you can write with clarity, passion, and conviction.

▸ **Stage 4: Manifesting Your Dreams** (Chapters 10-12)

Finally, we'll turn dreams into reality. Whether your goal is to publish your work, complete a creative project, or enjoy writing as a form of personal expression, this stage is about taking action. You'll create a tangible plan for moving forward and turning your Freedom Dream into something tangible.

By the end of this book, you'll not only have written your way through personal challenges and triumphs but also have a clear vision of how to continue your journey as a writer and a liberated individual. The world is waiting for your voice, and this is the space where it begins.

How To Use Your Journal

First and foremost, dear writer, thank you. Picking up this journal is a testament to your commitment to self-discovery and creative expression.

So, how can you make the most of this experience?

1. Follow the Sequence

While freedom allows for choice, following the journal's sequence is recommended. Each chapter and exercise is thoughtfully designed to build upon the previous one, creating a layered journey of growth, insight, and transformation. Think of it as laying bricks for your creative foundation—each brick strengthens the foundation for the next level.

2. Take Your Time

This is not a race—be gentle with yourself and let each exercise unfold at its own pace. Some prompts may require quiet reflection, while others might spark an immediate rush of thoughts. Allow time for both. Give yourself permission to go at your own speed; there's no right or wrong way to approach this. Whether you write a few sentences or pages, the goal is to stay true to your voice and experience. Trust that each exercise will reveal what it needs to when you're ready.

3. To Do or Not To Do

While every exercise offers a new perspective and tool for your creative toolbox, you don't have to complete every single one. However, I encourage you to try them all, even the ones that feel challenging. Often, the exercises we resist the most are the ones that yield the most surprising and transformative revelations.

4. Your Journal, Your Rules

This is your space—make it your own. Scribble in the margins, doodle across the pages, use colorful pens or keep it minimal with black ink. Whether you prefer neat lines or free-flowing thoughts, this journal should reflect *you* in all your unique creativity. There are no wrong ways to write. I have included a few pages for you to make notes, but feel free to grab a separate notebook.

5. Revisit Often

Just like a layered book or poem, you may discover new meanings or insights when you revisit chapters or exercises over time. Your journal is a living document, evolving alongside you. Don't hesitate to revisit earlier sections—what you'll find upon reflection may surprise you.

6. Create your Sanctuary

Find your space and make it yours—carve out a personal spot for your writing sessions, whether it's a cozy corner by the window, during your morning train commute, under an old oak tree, or sneaking into a conference room at work for an hour of solitude. Ensure it's a place where your thoughts can flow freely and without judgment. Personalize it with items that inspire you—photographs, music, trinkets, or a soft blanket. Let this space become your sanctuary, where your creativity and reflections can thrive. The more room you give your mind to wander, the deeper your insights will grow.

Dear Writer, this journal was crafted with love and intention, gifted from my heart to yours. I hope that you not only harness its power but also savor every moment of this journey. May it be an enlightening experience that brings you closer to your most authentic, most liberated self. Enjoy the journey through *Not Just Words: Writing as Liberation*.

Chapter 1

The Essence of Freedom Dream Writing

Discover the power of writing as a tool for liberation and personal transformation.

Welcome, Freedom Dreamer!

Congratulations on moving into this transformative journey! I know you didn't pick up this journal to let it collect dust. You're here, fully committed, ready to embark on a path that promises change and self-liberation. And trust me—this is not your typical journal that starts with good intentions but ends up abandoned like a New Year's resolution by February. Nope! This time, you've got a guide and a friend right by your side, someone invested in your growth, cheering you on every step of the way. In this chapter, you'll learn what it means to dream beyond limits, using writing as a tool for self-discovery and expression. By the end of this chapter, you'll have begun to unlock the door to your inner world, where your authentic voice waits to be set free.

The Pen as Revolution: How Literature Fuels Liberation

The art of writing has long been a sanctuary for the silenced, a weapon for revolutionaries, and a canvas for dreamers. Across centuries, ink has become the tool for dismantling oppression, questioning entrenched power systems, and envisioning worlds where justice, equality, and freedom reign. Writing records history—it shapes it.

Liberation theories, born from an unrelenting desire to break free from chains—societal norms, political tyranny, or the prisons of the mind—have consistently found their most resonant voices in literature. With his unflinching prose, James Baldwin painted an indelible portrait of racial injustice in America. With her soaring verses, Maya Angelou sang the song of resilience and freedom in the face of adversity. Through his revolutionary pedagogy, Paulo Freire used words to awaken consciousness, fanning the flames of liberation in the hearts of both young and old. Through these works, literature extended beyond an art form into a battleground for justice.

In this complex of liberation, voices from around the globe have played a pivotal role. For instance, Nigerian author Chimamanda Ngozi Adichie threads narratives of cultural identity and gender liberation through her works. *Half of a Yellow Sun* and *Americanah* confront societal norms, challenging readers to reexamine identity, power, and freedom. Her stories, rooted in her unique cultural heritage, resonate universally, echoing the shared human pursuit of dignity and liberty.

Likewise, through the alchemy of magical realism in *Midnight's Children*, Salman Rushdie interlaces freedom and imagination together into a force that defies convention. His worlds, where fantasy and reality collide, push readers to rethink the boundaries of cultural and societal norms, making us question what is possible in our pursuit of liberation.

However, liberation literature isn't only found in the celebrated works of literary giants. It thrives in the margins—in the diaries tucked away in forgotten attics, in unsent letters and whispered stories passed down through generations. These personal, often unseen, narratives carry the same power. They, too, tell stories of resistance, survival, and rebirth. These are the echoes of voices that refused to be silenced, each word a testament to human endurance and the desire for freedom.

And that, dear writer, is the legacy you are walking into. Your words—grand or quietly whispered—join this chorus of liberation, where every sentence is a step toward a more just and freer world.

If there's a book that you want to read, but it hasn't been written yet, then you must write it.

— TONI MORRISON

Outcomes for Chapter 1

By the end of this chapter, you will have:

1. Defined your personal "why" for writing.
2. Created a safe space for your Freedom Dream Writing practice.
3. Established a deeper understanding of how Freedom Dreaming applies to your writing.
4. Taken the first step toward using your writing as a tool for personal and collective liberation.

Overall Objective: These exercises are designed to help you use your imagination to envision a just and equitable future and bring those dreams to life through your words. By the end, you'll experience how your writing can inspire real change and serve as a tool for liberation—both for yourself and for others.

Exercise 1: Creating Your Sanctuary

Spot Hunt: Spend 15 minutes finding your perfect writing spot. This could be any place where you feel at peace and inspired—a cozy corner, a sunlit nook, or even beneath the open sky. Wherever it is, this space will become your sanctuary.

Inventory Check: Create a list of items that will make this space uniquely yours. Whether it's a favorite pen, a soft cushion, a cup of tea, or calming music, these elements will become vital to your writing ritual, helping you connect with your creative energy.

Sketch Your Space: If you're feeling creative (and even if you're not!), sketch a simple drawing of your sanctuary in your journal. This visual reminder will help solidify your commitment to this journey and make your space feel sacred.

Exercise 2: Your Identify, Your Passion, Your Why

Ask yourself: What issue truly ignites my fire? Is it racial equality? Gender rights? Climate justice? Economic fairness? Take a few moments to write down the issue that speaks most powerfully to you. This is the starting point for your freedom dream.

Exercise 3: Freedom Dream Brainstorm

Let's get those creative gears turning! Spend 10-15 minutes brainstorming what the world would look like if this issue were resolved. Go big—don't limit yourself. Reflect on questions like:

- What does this transformed future look like?
- How are people's lives different?
- What systems and structures are in place to ensure justice and equality?

This is your dream world, so don't be afraid to envision the extraordinary.

Exercise 4: Visualize and Reflect

Close your eyes and immerse yourself in the dream you've just brainstormed. Imagine living in this future—what do you see? What do you feel? What are the sights, sounds, and emotions of this new world? Spend another 10-15 minutes visualizing this dream, then write a one-page reflection capturing every detail. Let your senses guide you as you write this dream to life.

Exercise 5: Writing Your Freedom Dream

Now, it's time to bring it all together. Using your brainstorming and reflection, write at least a one-page narrative or essay that describes your dream future. Use the following prompts to guide your writing:

- "In my dream world, the issue of [your chosen issue] has been resolved by..."
- "Life in this future looks like..."
- "To get here, we took these steps and actions..."
- "The community played a crucial role by..."
- "This vision inspires me because..."

Let your imagination run wild, and don't hold back—this is where your freedom dream takes shape.

Final Thoughts

At this point in your journey, you've begun to unearth the stories and experiences that have shaped you. You've taken your first step in self-discovery, peeling back the layers that have hidden your true self. Think about how far you've come already—what aspects of your identity have you uncovered that were once buried? Your next step is all about giving that self a voice.

Chapter 2

Embracing Your True Identity

Explore the depth and complexities of your identity and how it shapes your writing.

Identity & Liberation: Unmasking the Self

Unmasking your true self is an act of **radical Freedom Dreaming**. This transformative process involves releasing the expectations, labels, and roles imposed by society, unveiling a version of yourself that exists beyond these constructs. Picture shedding the protective layers you've worn for years and confronting the reflection of who you genuinely are—not the version the world expects you to be. This is where the power of Freedom Dreaming begins to work—right here, as you reclaim your narrative and design your future according to your own values.

As you release the pressure of these external expectations, your writing voice will naturally grow in strength and authenticity, infused with the raw honesty of embracing your core identity.

James Baldwin powerfully stated, "Not everything that is faced can be changed, but nothing can be changed until it is faced." Baldwin, like many writers before him, confronted his own identity in a world that often tried to silence or distort his truth. He understood the importance of facing hard truths about our internalized beliefs and limitations. In this chapter, you'll confront the stories that have shaped you and begin to imagine the possibilities of who you can become once those limitations are stripped away. **Freedom Dreaming** empowers you to envision the most unfiltered essence or the core of who you are.

Defining Yourself Beyond Society's Labels

Zora Neale Hurston boldly proclaimed, "I am not tragically colored." Hurston's words, like her life, disrupted the narratives imposed upon Black women during her time. In her groundbreaking novel, Their Eyes Were Watching God, her protagonist, Janie, embarks on a journey of self-discovery that challenges societal norms. Janie's story is about survival, but more importantly, it's about joy, self-worth, and claiming the right to live unapologetically. She refuses to be defined by the limitations placed on her as a woman, as a Black woman, or as someone confined by her relationships.

Just as Hurston defied the labels thrust upon her, you too can begin the process of unraveling the stories that others have placed on your shoulders. The journey to your most authentic self begins with recognizing the burdens you carry—those imposed by society and the ones you've internalized over time. By confronting these labels and limitations, you create space for your true identity to emerge, even when others can't yet see that vision.

Unpacking Your Identity: A Journey of Self-Discovery

We all carry a figurative backpack of identity—stuffed with pieces of who we are, shaped by our memories, our cultures, and our experiences. Some of these fragments are treasures—moments of triumph, joy and stories that highlight our inner fortitude. But others are burdens—stories we've been carrying for so long, perhaps unknowingly, that they weigh us down.

Now is the time to unzip that backpack, lay everything out, and examine what's inside. You might not love everything you find, but this isn't about judgment—it's a journey of self-discovery. Think of this process as decluttering your soul. As you sift through the contents, some items will feel heavy representing the labels or roles you've held onto that no longer serve you. Others might shine with the spark of joy or strength, reminding you of your impact. By shedding these outdated stories, you create room for new possibilities, new dreams, and a more authentic version of yourself to emerge.

Journal Prompt:

Take a moment to visualize this backpack. What are some of the items you see inside? Are there any heavy objects weighing you down—perhaps a story you were told about your worth that still lingers? What treasures do you find that still bring you joy?

Now, imagine yourself removing one heavy item and setting it aside. How does it feel to release this burden? What does it make space for in your life and in your creative expression?

Questions for Reflection:

Ask yourself:

- **Who am I beyond the labels society has given me?**
- **Which roles have I chosen willingly, and which have been imposed upon me?**

- ▸ **What beliefs or biases have I internalized that might hold me back from dreaming fully?**
- ▸ **What am I still carrying that no longer represents my identity?**
- ▸ **Am I living authentically, or am I shaped by who I think I should be?**

You're not criticizing yourself for what you're not. You're asking, as Hurston and Baldwin did, **"How can I bring forth the true essence of who I am?"** As you sift through the fragments of your identity, imagine how much lighter you will feel once you free yourself from outdated narratives. You're opening pathways for your most authentic, vibrant self to emerge. This is the very essence of **Freedom Dreaming** in action: shedding the load of the past, embracing your true identity, and giving your future the space it needs to grow.

Wielding Emotions as Liberation

In today's fight for identity and self-liberation, the concept of unmasking is more relevant than ever. In her work, *Eloquent Rage,* feminist scholar and writer Dr. Brittney Cooper redefines anger not as something to suppress but as a tool for liberation. She argues that Black women, in particular, are often expected to suppress their emotions to fit into society's narrow definitions of acceptability. But Cooper flips this narrative on its head, reclaiming rage as a powerful force for change.

"Rage becomes a kind of superpower," she writes, "a force for making change in the world and an affirmation of Black women's right to exist unapologetically." For Cooper, embracing one's emotions fully—whether it's anger, joy, or sorrow—is an act of radical self-love and resistance. Her work is a testament to the idea that unmasking isn't just about revealing your identity; it's about wielding that identity as a force for **collective liberation**.

Just like Freedom Dreaming, Cooper's reframing of rage teaches us that our full range of emotions can serve as a source of power. Whether it's rage against systemic oppression or joy in the face of adversity, our emotions are essential tools in creating new narratives of freedom and self-worth. In this way, unmasking your genuine essence becomes more than personal liberation—it becomes a radical act that helps shape the world around you.

The Ancestry of Words: How the Past Shapes Your Writing

Now that we've explored the inner depths of self, let's shift our focus to the broader scope of history and ancestry. The stories we tell—and how we write—don't exist in isolation. They are often shaped by the voices of the past, by the traditions, wisdom, and legacies passed down through generations. Our words carry reminisce of those who came before us, making our writing a continuation of a much larger story.

Consider the profound tradition of Indigenous storytelling. These narratives are more than just tales—they pulse with life lessons about the interconnectedness of humans and nature, the value of community, and spiritual wisdom. Indigenous stories reflect a collective liberation, one that is deeply rooted in relationships—with the earth, with each other, and with the cosmos. Through these stories, freedom transcends the individual, offering insights into living harmoniously within a larger world.

Similarly, the rich oral traditions of Africa preserve cultural identity and communal liberation. From the griots of West Africa to the praise singers of Southern Africa, storytelling serves as the lifeblood of cultural preservation. Griots, for example, do more than recount history—they embody it. As custodians of memory, griots weave the past with the present, preserving their people's struggles, victories, and values. Each story told, each song sung, is a thread in the fabric of collective liberation—a reminder that freedom is both personal and communal, tied to the spirit of those who came before us. This tradition of honoring ancestors through words reminds us that every story we write carries ancestral force.

Our Writing as a Continuation of Ancestral Voices

Regardless of your heritage, your writing continues in these ancestral voices. Your words carry the wisdom of your grandparents, the inner power of your ancestors, and the cultural heritage woven into the fabric of your identity. Every piece you write is influenced by family gatherings, whispered lessons from elders, or stories passed down through generations—both spoken and unspoken.

Think about this: writing is more than just an act of self-expression—it is a living testament to the voices that shaped you, the history that informs you, and the culture that breathes through you. Just as you have unraveled the personal labels that once defined you through Freedom Dreaming, you now have the opportunity to tap into the ancestral threads that continue to shape your writing. These threads add layers of depth, richness, and connection to your craft.

As you write, consider the traditions, rituals, and stories you grew up with. These memories might surface as a particular phrase, a family saying, or even a scene that embodies the values passed down to you. How do these ancestral voices show up in your work? Do they inform the structure of your stories, the characters you create, or the themes you explore?

Sit with these Questions:

- **What stories from my past still resonate with my present self?**
- **Have dreams or aspirations been passed down to me, consciously or unconsciously?**
- **How has my ancestry—my family history, my culture—influenced how I approach writing?**

With every story you uncover, with every realization about where your voice comes from, you enrich your writing. It's like discovering that the song you've been humming is a melody passed down through generations or realizing that the laugh you share with loved ones mirrors the joy of your ancestors. In this sense, your writing becomes a continuation of a rich tradition—your personal act of Freedom Dreaming that connects the past, present, and future.

Freedom Dreaming and Ancestral Legacy

Just as Freedom Dreaming calls for imagining a liberated future, the ancestral stories embedded in your writing offer you the foundation to build upon. They remind you that you are not only the storyteller but also the inheritor of countless voices that dreamed of freedom long before you. By honoring these voices, your writing does more than tell a story—it reclaims, reshapes, and dreams of a future where your ancestors' hopes and sacrifices come to fruition.

In the same way that Brittney Cooper redefines rage as a liberatory force, the ancestral voices in your writing offer you the power to redefine your narrative. Whether through joy or rage, these ancestral stories allow you to engage in a radical act of creation rooted in history but unbound by the limitations of the past. Through your words, you honor where you've come from and carve out new possibilities for where you and future generations are headed.

I will fight for my hard-won blitheness and continue to choose joy.

— ZORA NEALE HURSTON

Outcomes for Chapter 2

By the end of this chapter, you will have:

1. Recognized the masks you wear and reflected on your true, unfiltered self.
2. Connected with your ancestry and understood its influence on your writing.
3. Started shedding societal expectations to embrace your authentic identity.
4. Taken actionable steps to live and write with greater freedom and self-liberation.

Overall Objective: As you move into Chapter 2, recognize the transformation already stirring within you. Each word you've written, each moment of reflection, is a step deeper into Freedom Dream Writing. The following exercises will guide you through an exploration of your identity, ancestry, and the masks you've worn, inviting you to confront and address those societal expectations that no longer work for you.

Exercise 1: The Mask and the Mirror

Objective: To reveal the layers of your true identity by examining the masks you wear for the world versus the self you see when no one is watching. This exercise will help you begin to release the societal expectations that have kept you from embracing YOU.

Step 1: Reflect on Your Mask. Take a few moments to reflect on the roles or personas you adopt in different areas of life. Do you show up differently at work than at home? What version of yourself do you present to friends versus strangers? For five minutes, jot down the various "masks" you wear in different situations or with different people. These could be personality traits, behaviors, or even attitudes that you've felt compelled to display.

Step 2: Who Are You Without the Mask? Now, ask yourself, who are you when no one else is around? When the world isn't watching, how do you truly feel about yourself, your dreams, and your values? For 10 minutes, write freely about the person behind the masks—your raw, unfiltered self. Don't hold back. This is your chance to be real without judgment. You might discover emotions, thoughts, or dreams you've been keeping hidden. Let them surface.

Step 3: The Mirror Moment. Find a mirror, or simply close your eyes and imagine yourself standing before one. Take a moment to look at yourself. Who do you see? What parts of yourself do you want to honor more in your day-to-day life? What aspects of your reflection make you feel proud, and which parts feel neglected or hidden?

Step 4: Letting Go of Expectations. On a new page, write a list of expectations—either from society, family, or yourself—that no longer serve you. These might be pressure to be a certain way, meet certain standards, or fit into a mold you've outgrown. For each one, note down how you can begin to release it, freeing yourself to show up as the truest version of you.

Reflection: As you complete this exercise, notice the emotions that arise. Was it challenging to identify the masks you wear? Did you feel a sense of relief or discomfort as you reflect on yourself? This process is an invitation to begin peeling back those layers and advancing into your genuine self. This empowers you not just as a writer but as a fully realized individual—unbound by the expectations of s of e expectations of others, and live and write from a place of truth.

Exercise 2: Ancestral Echoes & Personal Legacies

Objective: Connect with the echoes of your ancestry, personal experiences, and the communities that have shaped you. Understand how these influences guide your writing and your dreams.

10-Minute Reflective Writing: Write a short piece inspired by a story, tradition, or experience from your heritage. This could be a folktale passed down through generations, a cultural practice, or a family ritual that holds meaning for you. As you write, reflect on how this story connects to your identity and influences your current writing aspirations. What lessons or values does it carry? How do these ancestral sounds echoes shape your desire to tell your story?

Consider how your ancestors' resilience, creativity, or struggles have influenced the stories you feel compelled to share. Remember: your writing continues their legacy—a voice among many, contributing to the tapestry of history and culture.

Actionable Step: After completing your reflective writing, take a small action to engage further with your ancestry. Reach out to a family member for a conversation about your heritage, research a cultural practice, or revisit a significant family story. Let this connection ground you in the wisdom of those who came before you.

Exercise 3: The Liberation Gala

Objective: Reflect on the internal struggles and societal pressures that have shaped your identity and confront the "masks" you've worn. This exercise invites you to shed these expectations and envision a life where you live freely, unburdened by societal labels.

Writing Prompt: In a world not far from our own, an annual tradition exists: The Liberation Gala. It's no ordinary event—it's where people wear masks sculpted from the societal, cultural, and personal expectations they carry. The heavier the expectation, the heavier the mask.

This year, a shimmering invitation arrives at your doorstep. The theme, etched in gold, reads: "To Unveil, To Liberate, To Triumph."

Standing before a grand mirror, you see a collection of masks—each representing a burden you've carried: The Pleaser, The Overachiever, The Silent Strength, The Caretaker. With the Gala fast approaching, you realize: Who am I when I free myself from these expectations?

Instructions:

1. Confront the Masks: Write an essay exploring the societal, cultural, or personal masks you've worn. How have these masks shaped your identity? Which ones were placed upon you by external forces, and which ones did you choose to wear? What expectations have they imposed?

2. Liberation: Reflect on the moment you decide to remove these masks. How does it feel to free yourself from the weight of these roles? Describe the emotional and physical release as you step into your liberated self—unburdened, free, and empowered.

3. The Liberation Gala: Picture yourself arriving at The Liberation Gala unmasked and triumphant. Describe your grand entrance. Who is by your side? What do you see, feel, hear, and smell? Celebrate this victory. How do you honor this newfound freedom?

4. A Life of Liberation: Conclude with your vision for life without these societal chains. How will you nurture this freedom? How will you ensure that your future is defined by your authentic self rather than the expectations of others? What steps will you take to protect and celebrate this liberation every day?

Reflection: This exercise names the masks and celebrates the freedom that comes with removing them. Embrace the joy, the lightness, and the strength that liberation brings. Let your words become a declaration of your triumph, a testament to the freedom you've chosen.

Final Thoughts

Now that you've connected with your ancestral stories, you understand how deeply your past influences your present voice. You're standing on the shoulders of your ancestors, ready to write the next chapter of your lineage. This understanding empowers your words with more meaning and purpose as you continue your journey.

As you move forward, let these words constantly remind you of your strength, resilience, and unyielding potential. You hold the pen, and with it, you can write your destiny. Keep writing, keep rising, and let your story unfold as it was always meant to—on your terms.

Chapter 3

Confronting the Critic Within

Learn to overcome internal criticism and self-doubt to unlock your true writing potential.

In Chapter 2, we began tapping into the power of your voice, but now it's time to confront the unwelcome guest that often sneaks in uninvited: the internal critic. Yep, we all have that voice—one minute, it's casually telling you you're not good enough, and the next, it's doing a full-on roast of your dreams. It's time to shut that voice down and reclaim the narrative. In this chapter, we'll confront the harshest voice you'll ever face: your inner critic. Together, we'll explore where this voice comes from and how you can turn it from an obstacle into an ally. By the end, you'll have the tools to quiet your self-doubt and reclaim your power.

Understanding the Internal Critic

Let's face it: that voice of doubt didn't just appear out of thin air. It's a culmination of past experiences, societal pressures, and personal insecurities, all bundled together in an overly critical package. But don't worry— we're not here to banish the critic altogether (because, let's be honest, it's probably not going anywhere). Instead, we will transform it from a harsh judge into a constructive co-conspirator for your creative growth. Liberation is waiting on the other side of this internal battle, and trust me—it's worth the fight.

The Roots of the Internal Critic

So, where does this internal critic come from? Understanding its origins is the first step toward transforming it. Here are some of the root causes:

1. Early Life Experiences:

Early life experiences have a profound impact on shaping our inner dialogue, often giving rise to an internal critic that can hinder our journey toward liberation through writing. Perhaps you had a teacher who dismissed your ideas, making you feel invisible, or a supervisor who scoffed at your ideas (remember mine from the introduction? yeah, we are still giving that person the side eye), or you grew up in a household where perfection was the standard and mistakes were met with disappointment. These experiences plant seeds of self-doubt, fostering an inner voice that questions your worth and capabilities.

Brené Brown, a researcher known for her work on shame and vulnerability, emphasizes how our formative years contribute to the stories we tell ourselves. In her book *"The Gifts of Imperfection,"* she explains that when we're conditioned to believe our efforts are never enough, we internalize a sense of inadequacy. This internal critic becomes a constant companion, whispering that our words aren't valuable, that our stories don't matter.

This critical inner voice can impede your writing by instilling fear and self-doubt. It tells you to hold back, to second-guess every word, to question the legitimacy of your own experiences. Instead of writing freely and authentically, you might find yourself trapped in a cycle of perfectionism and silence, unable to express the truths that are yearning to be told.

Understanding that this internal critic is a learned response—not an inherent part of who you are—is a crucial step toward liberation. Recognizing its roots allows you to challenge its narrative. As Brené Brown suggests, embracing vulnerability and imperfection is key to quieting this voice. By practicing self-compassion and reframing your inner dialogue, you can begin to transform the critic from a barrier into a bridge that leads to deeper self-understanding and authentic expression.

When you confront and heal from these early influences, you open up space for your true voice to emerge. Your writing becomes a tool for liberation—a way to reclaim your story and assert your place in the world. By acknowledging and addressing the roots of your internal critic, you empower yourself to move beyond self-imposed limitations and write with the freedom and confidence that reflect your true self.

2. Societal Expectations:

Let's not pretend that society doesn't pile on the pressure—because it does. Everywhere you look, an endless loop of perfection is being sold, from social media highlight reels to cultural expectations that dictate how we "should" present ourselves. Writing, like any creative pursuit, gets swept into this madness. We see other people sharing their polished final drafts, book deals, or Insta-perfect "writing spaces," and suddenly, that internal critic perks up, whispering: "You'll never measure up to that." But here's the truth: you're not playing the same game, and nobody's keeping score but you.

Society pushes this idea that to be worthy, you need to meet specific standards. But whose standards are those, really? It's a game designed to make you feel like you're falling behind, like you'll never quite be "enough." Social media makes it worse by magnifying the gap between the real, raw you and the curated perfection of others. It traps us in a cycle of self-doubt, making it nearly impossible to let our creativity breathe. We start worrying that our words aren't *enough*—not edgy enough, not commercial enough, not "important" enough—when, in truth, the act of creating is inherently **ENOUGH.**

3. Personal Insecurities:

We've all faced those nagging fears—the ones that whisper we're not good enough, smart enough, or talented enough. Maybe it's the persistent belief that we have nothing important or original to say, that our words will never make an impact. Or perhaps it's the fear that what we write will never live up to the lofty expectations we've set for ourselves, let alone anyone else's. These insecurities, whether small or overwhelming, feed the internal critic an endless supply of ammunition. And believe me, it loves to use every single bullet.

But here's the thing: personal insecurities are completely normal. They're part of being human, and they don't have to stop you. It's tempting to think that successful writers are somehow immune to these doubts, that they glide through their creative process without the constant baggage of uncertainty dragging them down. But I promise you, that's not true. The difference is that they've learned to keep writing *through* the insecurity, not without it. They understand that doubt is part of the process, not a barrier to success.

Think about that. Even the most seasoned writers, the ones whose words move mountains and shape conversations, face the same insecurities you do. They, too, sit down at their desks with the nagging voice of doubt lurking in the background. The voice that says, *Is this good enough? Will anyone care?* But they write anyway. They push through the fear because they've learned something crucial: doubts are part of the process, not a sign that they should stop.

They don't define your talent, and they sure as hell don't dictate your worth. The critic's voice is loud, yes, but it's not the final word. You get to decide what's real.

When those insecurities start creeping in, take a step back. Recognize the critic for what it is—a voice that thrives on fear. But remember, you're in control. That critic doesn't know your potential. It doesn't know the power of your words. You get to decide how much space you give that voice and how much influence it has over your writing. And more importantly, you have the power to keep writing, even with the doubt sitting beside you on your couch.

Remember, the path to becoming a writer isn't a straight line paved with confidence. It's a winding road filled with moments of self-doubt, fear, and hesitation. But it's also filled with breakthroughs, with moments when you push through the uncertainty and find your voice on the other side. That's what separates those who dream of writing from those who actually do it—the willingness to move forward, even when the doubts are loud.

So, when you feel that familiar wave of uncertainties rising, don't retreat. Lean into it. Acknowledge it for what it is—a fleeting thought, a passing feeling. It's not who you are. Then sit down, pick up your pen, and write anyway. Write with the doubt sitting next to you and show yourself that you don't need permission to create. You already have everything you need within you.

The Impact of the Internal Critic

Let's get real about what happens when you let that inner critic run wild. It doesn't just stay in the background—it digs in, plants roots, and affects every aspect of your creative process. If left unchecked, the critic does more than slow you down; it can completely derail your writing journey; trust me, I know. Here are some ways the internal critic manifests itself; which one resonates with you?

- **Paralysis by Analysis:**
  Have you ever found yourself sitting in front of a blank page or cursor blinking accusingly, and your mind racing through a million "what ifs"? What if this is terrible? What if no one likes it? What if I'm just not cut out for this? That's *paralysis by analysis*— the inner critic's most insidious weapon. You get so caught up in pre-editing or second-guessing yourself that you never even get to the writing part. Instead of letting the words flow, you dissect every potential phrase before it even has a chance to land on the page. It's like trying to drive with the parking brake on—you're stuck in place, spinning your wheels, but going nowhere. The fear of producing something "not good enough" stops you from producing *anything* at all.

- **Creativity on Lockdown:**
  When your internal critic has the loudest voice in the room, creativity doesn't just shrink—it goes into hiding. Instead of allowing yourself to explore bold, new ideas or take creative risks, you retreat to the safety of what's already familiar. You stick to the safe zone, the tried-and-true, because the inner critic whispers, "Don't go too far outside the lines. Don't embarrass yourself." The result? Your writing becomes stifled, predictable, and worse—uninspired. You lose the joy of experimentation, and instead of expanding your creative boundaries, you shrink them down to what feels safe and manageable. Creativity, by its very nature, thrives in the unknown, the messy, and the risk-taking. But when your internal critic is in

charge, it builds a cage around that creativity, locking down your potential before it can stretch its wings.

▸ **Lower Self-Esteem:**

The internal critic is that persistent voice whispering, "You're not enough." We've all encountered it, and it can be overwhelming. However, it's crucial to understand that this voice does not define you. When you internalize these criticisms, they begin to chip away at your self-esteem. Suddenly, it's not just that your writing needs improvement—*you* need improvement. You start to doubt your abilities, not just as a writer but as a person capable of expressing themselves. This erosion of confidence makes it even harder to sit down and write because, deep down, the critic has convinced you that whatever you create will never measure up. It becomes a vicious cycle: the more you let the critic dictate your thoughts, the more your self-esteem suffers, and the harder it becomes to believe in the worth of your voice.

As mentioned, and I feel worth emphasizing, if left unchecked, the internal critic stifles your creative output and rewrites your entire narrative of self-worth. It's the ultimate saboteur, and its effects go far beyond a single writing session. The good news? You can shut it down, reclaim your creativity, and regain control of your narrative. It's time to turn down the volume on that internal critic. Here are ways to do so:

Strategies for Silencing the Critic

1. Acknowledge the Critic's Presence

First, recognize when the critic shows up. Just becoming aware of it can loosen its grip. When those negative thoughts start creeping in, pause and take note: "Oh, there you are again." Awareness is the first step in breaking the pattern.

2. Challenge Negative Thoughts

Ask yourself: Is this criticism based on fact, or is it just fear talking? More often than not, it's the latter. Replace negative thoughts with positive affirmations.

Pro tip: Write your affirmations down and stick them on your mirror, desk, or wherever you need them most.

3. Set Realistic Expectations

Let go of perfection. Spoiler alert: you'll never reach it. Aim for growth, not flawlessness. As Salvador Dalí wisely said, "Have no fear of perfection—you'll never reach it." Progress is the goal.

4. Build a Support Squad

Share your work with a trusted group of friends, mentors, or fellow writers. Feedback doesn't have to be scary—it can be empowering. The right people will lift you up, not tear you down. But we also have to brace ourselves for that one person in our squad who will intentionally criticize. Take their feedback with grace, and remember, not all critique is meant to discourage—sometimes, it's an opportunity to grow. Surround yourself with those who understand your vision and can push you constructively, and always remember, *you* decide what resonates and what doesn't.

5. Practice Self-Compassion

Let's flip the script. Instead of criticizing yourself, treat yourself with kindness. Celebrate the small victories, like finishing a paragraph or just sitting down to write. Research from Kristin Neff shows that practicing self-compassion leads to lower levels of anxiety and higher emotional resilience. So, be kind to yourself; you're doing great.

6. Embrace Mindfulness

Techniques like deep breathing, meditation, or a walk can help reduce the noise of the inner critic. Mindfulness helps clear the way between you and your thoughts, allowing you to focus on the task at hand.

7. Maintain a Writing Routine –

This one is a bit longer because it was (and is) something that I struggled with the most, and I offer this to those who are struggling the same way.

Consistency is the foundation of any successful writing practice. What I learned is that it is less about writing for hours on end or hitting an arbitrary word count and more about showing up. Whether it's 10 minutes every morning before the chaos of the day begins or an hour on the weekends when the house is quiet, the important thing is *starting*. The act of showing up, day after day, is what will set your foundation as a writer. Over time, the habit of writing will take root, and the critic's grip will loosen. The more you write, the less space there is for self-doubt and criticism to interfere. The rhythm of writing becomes a part of your daily life, and with every word, the critic's voice fades just a bit more.

Listen, I'm not about to pretend this is some utopian setup where you'll always have uninterrupted hours to devote to writing, while the world stands still waiting for you to finish that chapter or prose or page. Shit happens. Sometimes routines get broken. Kids need attention, pets demand walks, work deadlines pop up, or maybe you just get sucked into a *Law & Order* binge (no judgment here!). So, maybe you miss a day or even a week, and that's when the inner critic shows up, smug, condescending and loud: *"See? I told you aren't serious about this. A real writer wouldn't have let this happen. A real writer writes 10,589 words every day while churning butter and saving cats from trees, with no excuses. What's wrong with you?"* You know that voice. It simply loves to remind you of all the ways you're falling short.

Self-compassion, my friend, is your secret weapon in this part of your writing journey. So, you missed a day—or, heck, maybe even a week? Guess what? The world didn't end, and your progress didn't vanish into thin air. You're still a writer, and the work you've done is still gold. What really matters is getting yourself back to the page. Real writers aren't those perfect creatures who never stumble—they're the ones who trip, fall, and then get back up, dust off their pants, and say, "Well, that didn't go as planned!"

And hey, when guilt starts creeping in, tell it to take a seat. Give yourself some grace and dive back in. The real magic is in the habit of coming back, even when you feel like you're writing with two left hands. Sure, the critic in your head might start yelling like an over-caffeinated sports coach, but don't let that stop you. Keep writing, even if it feels like you're wrangling words like a cat chasing a laser pointer. Every time you return, you're proving to yourself that you've got what it takes to keep going. So, dust off that keyboard and let's do this—you've got this!

And if you're curious about the psychology behind habits, I highly recommend *The Power of Habit* by Charles Duhigg. This book dives into how small, consistent actions can reshape your life and craft. Another excellent resource is *Atomic Habits* by James Clear, which offers practical strategies for building sustainable routines, particularly for creatives. Both books can offer valuable insights into how to make consistency a natural part of your writing life, So, remember this: routines will break, and the critic will get louder, but none of that defines your worth or your ability as a writer. What defines you is your willingness to show up again, to put pen to paper even after a setback, and to keep pushing forward, one imperfect word at a time.

Breaking Free: From Criticism to Liberation

Now that we've identified the internal critic as the voice that tries to hold us back, it's time to shift our focus to transforming it into a tool for growth. Instead of revisiting its origins, let's go into actionable ways to quiet it when it rears its head and turn that doubt into determination.

And remember: Vulnerability isn't weakness—it's courage. It's the act of standing face-to-face with your fears and daring to write anyway. That's where the magic happens. Each wall you break down makes space for a new story, a new dream, and a louder, more powerful voice.

Not everything that is faced can be changed, but nothing can be changed until it is faced.

– JAMES BALDWIN

Outcomes for Chapter 3

By the end of this chapter, you will have:

1. Identified the roots and impact of your inner critic.
2. Learned practical strategies to challenge and quiet that negative voice.
3. Gained tools to cultivate self-compassion and build creative strides.
4. Empowered yourself to break free from self-doubt and embrace vulnerability in your writing.

Overall Objective: This exercise aims to help writers recognize the critic that often shadows their artistic journey, understand where these critical voices originate, and develop strategies to face them with resilience. By doing so, writers can transform their inner critic from a source of self-doubt into a constructive force, fostering artistic and personal growth.

Exercise: Voices in the Auditorium – Confronting Your Vulnerability

Prompt: Imagine standing in a vast auditorium, bathed in the harsh glare of a spotlight. Every seat is filled, each face reflecting a different chapter of your life—family members, friends, mentors, peers, and even strangers you've never met. The silence suffocates as you finish reading the last line of your most intimate piece of writing. The words linger in the air, vulnerable and raw.

Then, from the farthest corner of the room, a voice pierces through the stillness. It's sharp, direct, and calls out your deepest artistic insecurity, echoing for all to hear.

The voice declares, "_______________________," and at that moment, your heart sinks. It feels as though the room itself has grown heavier, pressing down on your chest, threatening to swallow you whole.

Dialogue with the Critic: This is when you face your critic, even if that voice is coming from within. Write a dialogue between you and this faceless critic. Address their comment head-on but without giving in to anger or defensiveness. Instead, explain the intention and emotion behind your art. How would you defend or explain your work while remaining grounded in your creative truth?

Consider the following questions as you write:

1. Identify the Criticism:
- What part of your writing or creative process is closest to your heart? Is it a personal story, a risky style choice, or a subject you feel deeply about?
- What vulnerable aspect of your work does the critic's comment attack? Recognize the sensitivity of this area, as it's likely something you guard closely.

2. Immediate Response:
- What was your gut reaction when you heard the criticism? Did you freeze? Did you want to flee the stage or burst into tears? Maybe you felt anger or a sharp pang of self-doubt?
- Elaborate on the emotions that rushed through you in that moment. Did you feel exposed, vulnerable, or even humiliated? Were you tempted to fight back, or did you retreat within yourself?

3. Trace Its Roots:
- Why does this particular criticism sting so profoundly? Can you trace its origin to a specific memory or person in your life?
- Was there an event in your past—a comment from a teacher, a parent, or a peer—that planted this seed of doubt in your mind? Reflect on how past experiences may have shaped your sensitivity to this critique.

4. Reflection & Realization:
- Now that the initial wave of emotion has passed, take a step back and reflect. What does this moment reveal about your own insecurities or growth areas? Did the critic touch on something that you've feared all along?

- Did this experience reaffirm your deepest fears, or did it illuminate areas where you might be able to improve or shift your perspective?

5. Turning Critique into Construct:

- Make a list of the critiques you heard. Be specific. Next to each criticism, write down how you can use it constructively. Is there truth to the critique that can help you refine your craft? How might you better communicate your vulnerability in the future?
- Use this opportunity to transform a painful moment into one of growth. How can you evolve as both an artist and a person, using the criticism as fuel for your creative fire?

Example of Dialogue:

Critic: "Your writing is too emotional. It feels indulgent like you're just spilling your personal baggage onto the page."

You: "I hear you. Yes, my writing is deeply emotional because my experiences are the core of my art. I've spent years trying to find the courage to express my feelings, knowing there's a risk in exposing my vulnerabilities. But isn't art meant to stir emotion? Isn't it meant to connect us in our rawest, most unguarded moments? My goal isn't to overwhelm but to offer something real that might resonate with others who've felt what I've felt. The vulnerability in my work is deliberate, not indulgent—it's an invitation to be human with me."

Final Thoughts

Congratulations! You've faced your inner critic head-on. By identifying the roots of your self-doubt and challenging those limiting beliefs, you've taken a huge step toward becoming a more confident, empowered writer. Keep these tools handy as we continue because they are vital to every part of this journey.

Chapter 4

Rising Empowerment

Empower yourself through writing and find inner strength and confidence in your voice.

Pause for a moment—yes, I mean right now. Close your eyes, take a deep breath, and think about how far you've come. Really think about it. We're one-third of the way through this journey together, and every step you've taken so far is proof of you wanting this. You've stared down your fears, silenced the inner critic (you know, the one that loves to show up uninvited), and you've embraced the power of your voice. That's no small thing, my friend. Give yourself credit—seriously. You've done the most challenging part by showing up. Now, we're going to take this journey to the next level by tapping into something even more transformative: empowerment.

Let's talk about that word for a minute—"empowerment." It's one of those terms that can feel overused, like something people throw around but rarely stop to explain. We're going to strip it down to what it truly means. Empowerment is recognizing your strength, owning it fully, and trusting in your worth without waiting for anyone else to tell you it's okay. It's about knowing deep in your bones that your voice, your story, and your presence in this world have value—without needing anyone's validation.

Empowerment means no more waiting for permission; instead, you are choosing to stand tall, even when others can't see what you're capable of. And trust me, some people won't see it. But guess what? That's their issue, not yours.

The word itself sounds grand, but self-empowerment is not always a grandiose, lightning-bolt moment where you suddenly feel like your favorite Marvel Comic hero. It's often quieter and more subtle. It shows up in the choices you make, day by day, sometimes minute by minute. It's deciding that you're done letting anyone else dictate your story and owning that your existence, in and of itself, is valid. You don't need a gold star from the world to know you're enough. You're not just here to take up space— you're here because you belong. And nobody gets to tell you otherwise.

The other thing about empowerment that I have learned is that it doesn't come well-prepared on a silver platter. You must claim it for yourself. But the real beauty of it —it's been inside you all along. As you read these words right now, you already have it. All we're doing now is helping you unlock it and turn up its volume. Once you fully step into your power, there's nothing and no one to take it from you.

So, go ahead—take another deep breath. This path you're on? It's yours to shape. You're creating your own trail with every decision, every word, and every courageous act of standing in your truth.

Reclaiming Your Power: The Art of Rising

Maya Angelou once said, *"I love to see a young girl go out and grab the world by the lapels. Life's a bitch. You've got to go out and kick ass."* That's the vibe we're embracing in this chapter: owning your space and deciding for yourself that you matter. Empowerment starts the moment you stop waiting for anyone else's approval. The moment you realize the power has been in your hands the entire time. You are the author of your own life and in control of making your own decisions, and when you stop letting others define who you are and finally say, "No more."

I remember feeling boxed in by other people's expectations of who I should be. It wasn't until I stopped chasing their approval and turned inward that I asked myself, *What do I really want?* That I began to feel empowered. That shift didn't happen overnight, and it wasn't accompanied by fireworks or me shouting from the top of the Empire State Building, "LOOK AT ME, I'M EMPOWERED!"—though let's be honest, that would've been pretty epic. Instead, it was a quiet realization that crept up on me.

One day, when faced with a challenge, I noticed something had changed. I didn't react the way I used to. My mind, my heart, my confidence—even my tone—had shifted. My response was different. I was different. I wasn't that girl anymore. I was the woman, as Maya Angelou would say, grabbing the world by its labels and kicking ass for me.

It was one of those subtle "aha" moments, and I'm sure you've had them too—those quiet moments when you realize you've achieved a personal goal no one else can see, hear, taste, or feel but you. And in that moment, you smile to yourself, give yourself a little pat on the back, and maybe even reward yourself for doing the damn internal work. For me? That reward looks like a pint of Ben & Jerry's Half Baked.

Once you embrace your (em)power, you discover a freedom and peace that no one can take away. It's a freedom that comes from being aligned with your own truth, your power, and tenacity, not someone else's version of you. And that's what real empowerment looks like.

Empowerment: A Daily Practice

Think of empowerment like a muscle—you don't hit the gym once and expect to leave with rock-solid abs, right? Empowerment works the same way. Each day, you make a conscious decision to stand up for your own worth, even when doubt is knocking at your door.

A Daily Practice for Empowerment:

- **Start the day with intention**
  Each morning, set a small goal or affirmation that aligns with your values. Something like *Today, I honor my voice*, or *I am worthy of being seen and heard*. This simple practice trains your brain to focus on your personal worth.

- **Embrace the good days and the hard ones.**
  Some days, feeling empowered will feel effortless, like you're totally in sync with yourself. Other days, it'll feel like you're wading through mud—doubts creeping in, fear whispering in your ear. Keep showing up anyway. It's not about perfection; it's about persistence.

- **Take small, consistent steps.**
  It's easy to believe that empowerment comes from big, bold moves. In reality, it grows slowly, quietly, with those small, everyday actions. Whether it's speaking up in a meeting, setting a boundary, or honoring your need for rest, every action counts.

- **Claim your space**
  Stand tall, even when the ground feels shaky beneath you. Practice this by doing something daily that asserts your presence—whether that's sharing your thoughts openly, making a decision

based on what's right for you, or simply reminding yourself that you deserve to be here every single day.

▸ **Self-compassion breaks**

Research by Dr. Kristin Neff shows that self-compassion is a crucial part of empowerment. When self-doubt hits, take a moment to be kind to yourself. It could be as simple as saying, *This is hard, but I'm doing my best,* or *I'm allowed to take up space just as I am.*

▸ **Practice vulnerability**

Brené Brown's research in *The Gifts of Imperfection* highlights the connection between vulnerability and empowerment. Being vulnerable doesn't mean being weak—it means owning who you are, flaws and all. Take small steps to show up as your authentic self each day. This might look like expressing your true feelings or admitting when you need help.

Writing as Your Superpower

Let's talk about writing. Because if you're anything like me, writing is more than just a creative outlet. It's a superpower. Every time you sit down to write—be it a journal entry, a poem, or a stream of consciousness—you're shaping reality, defining your identity, and opening doors to possibilities that once felt out of reach. Writing is your ultimate tool for agency.

And it's not just me saying this—research backs it up. Dr. James Pennebaker's studies on expressive writing show that writing about your thoughts and feelings can reduce stress, improve mental health, and deepen self-awareness. Writing helps us process our experiences, heal from wounds, and gain clarity in our lives. It's a form of empowerment that comes from within—a way to reclaim your voice and step into your truth.

Reclaiming Your Narrative: Taking Back the Mic

No one else gets to write your story. It's yours and yours alone. Reclaiming your narrative is like taking back the mic at your own concert after someone else tried to steal the spotlight. This is your life. Your voice. Your truth. And no one can take that from you.

Throughout history, marginalized communities have turned to storytelling as a way to reclaim their power, voice, and rightful place in the world. For these communities, storytelling hasn't been a luxury; it's been a lifeline—a way to pass down wisdom, preserve culture, and resist oppression. Many authors from these backgrounds have broken molds, using their words as tools of empowerment, reclaiming narratives that were once taken from them.

This tradition of storytelling, whether spoken or written, has always served a deeper purpose; for many, it was about survival and creating change. From African oral traditions that passed wisdom down through generations to modern-day writers who challenge systems of oppression, stories have the power to transform not only individuals but entire societies. When you reclaim your own narrative, you're not just healing yourself—you're contributing to the collective empowerment of others.

Take Angie Thomas, for example. Writing in the 21st century, Thomas faced the challenge of addressing systemic racism and police brutality through her work. Her novel *The Hate U Give* gives voice to the Black Lives Matter movement, portraying the life of a young Black girl who witnesses the fatal shooting of her friend by police. Thomas didn't shy away from difficult topics; she confronted them head-on, reclaiming the narrative surrounding Black youth and communities. Her work resonates globally, standing as a testament to the power of telling your story authentically. She didn't wait for permission to share these truths; she wrote herself into the conversation, influencing countless readers and sparking meaningful dialogue.

Another contemporary author, Ocean Vuong, reclaims his narrative in a deeply personal way. As a Vietnamese-American poet and novelist, Vuong explores themes of identity, migration, and the complexities of family in his work. In his novel *On Earth We're Briefly Gorgeous*, he writes a letter to his mother who cannot read, delving into intergenerational trauma and the immigrant experience. Vuong's poetic prose challenges conventional storytelling and brings marginalized voices to the forefront. By sharing his unique perspective, he not only tells his own story but also gives voice to others who have felt unseen and unheard.

These writers—Angie Thomas and Ocean Vuong—have shown us what it looks like to take back the mic and reclaim the narrative. They faced criticism, opposition, and societal pressure to conform, yet they chose to write their truth anyway. They knew their voices mattered, and because they were brave enough to own their stories, they have inspired countless others to do the same.

So, how does this apply to you?

When you write your story—your real story—you are empowering yourself and reclaiming your narrative. You're saying that no one else gets to define who you are or what your experiences mean. You are taking control of the script. Whether it's through journaling, poetry, essays, or even conversations with trusted friends, telling your story is an act of empowerment. It's an assertion that your voice is valuable, your perspective is unique, and your truth deserves to be told.

I know by now you have heard this theme repeated throughout this chapter; that is intentional. EMPOWERMENT IS A PROCESS. Usain Bolt trained for years and years to run so he could run 100 meters in under nine seconds. Really sit with that. I know that in this microwave generation, the pressure can seem to want everything to happen overnight, but reclaiming your narrative doesn't have to happen all at once, and that's okay. You are allowed to begin with small, personal steps; you are allowed to find your rhythm and fine-tune your rhythm. It can look like finally admitting a truth you've been avoiding, writing about an experience you've been told isn't important, or simply allowing yourself to speak up when you've been conditioned to stay silent – I know what that feels like all too well. Every time you take back control of your story, no matter how small, you're reclaiming your power.

As Audre Lorde famously said, "Your silence will not protect you." So, take back the mic. Tell your story boldly, and without apology. Because when you do, you're not only giving voice to your own experience— you're helping others find the courage to do the same.

Rising to Meet Yourself

So, rise. Write. Own your voice, your story, your strength. The world may need your light, but more importantly—you need it. You deserve to stand in your power, not because someone else told you to, but because you know it's yours to claim.

Every word you write is a reminder that you are here, that you matter, and that your story deserves to be told. Empowerment doesn't come from anyone else—it comes from within. And with every word, you're not just telling a story—you're defining your place in this world. So, take up space. Because you, my friend, are unstoppable.

You may not control all the events that happen to you, but you can decide not to be reduced by them.

— MAYA ANGELOU

Outcomes for Chapter 4

By the end of this chapter, you will:

1. Recognize the intrinsic power you hold within your writing and how it empowers you to shape your narrative.
2. Understand the significance of reclaiming your voice and story, especially in a world that may try to silence it.
3. Develop a deeper connection to your empowerment through writing, recognizing the transformative power of your words.
4. Begin to see writing as an act of self-actualization that goes beyond just telling a story and becomes a tool for shaping your future.

Overall Objective: To harness the transformative power of writing, shifting from liberation to full actualization, grounded in the Freedom Dreaming journey. This is your moment to claim the pen, the power, and the path to the life you envision, guiding your voice from reflection to bold, fearless action.

Exercise 1: Affirmation Alchemy – Claiming Your Power

Description: Affirmations are not just feel-good phrases; they are potent declarations that shape who you are and who you are becoming. Writing affirmations is a radical act of Freedom Dreaming, where you envision your most empowered self and speak it into existence.

Action: Write down five affirmations that resonate deeply with your dreams, goals, and how you wish to perceive yourself. Make them personal, powerful, and reflective of the life you are building through your writing.

Examples:

- "I am resilient, capable, and worthy of every dream I pursue."
- "My voice holds power, and my story deserves to be heard."
- "Challenges fuel my growth, and when I face them, I emerge stronger each time."
- "I am the architect of my destiny, shaping it with each word I write."
- "I am unstoppable in my pursuit of joy, growth, and fulfillment."

Reflection: Why did you choose these affirmations? How do they align with the empowered self you're transitioning into? Reflect on the emotions they stir in you—what truths are you claiming, and what fears are you dismantling? Remember, writing these affirmations down is an act of radical Freedom Dreaming. By putting them to paper, you're not just reflecting—you're actively manifesting the person you are becoming. Keep them close; these are your guiding lights on this journey.

Exercise 2: Rewrite the Script – Reclaiming Your Narrative

Description: Everyone has a moment when someone else tries to define your story—casting doubt on your abilities, dreams, or worth. This exercise is about taking back the pen and rewriting the narrative from a place of empowerment and resilience.

Action: Think back to when someone else tried to write your story for you, casting doubt or limitations on your potential. Write down that negative narrative, then rewrite it from a place of strength and self-belief.

Prompt: Here's an example.

- Doubt: "You're not talented enough to make it in that industry."
- Reclaimed Narrative: "My talent is undeniable, and my creativity reshapes every space I enter."

Reflection: This exercise goes beyond rewriting one negative story by reclaiming your voice and declaring that no one else gets to define your path. Challenge those limiting beliefs and reshape them into narratives rooted in empowerment, resilience, and truth. Your story is yours to tell—write it on your terms.

Exercise 3: Power Paragraph – Progressing Into Your Future

Description: Envision a future where you've fully embraced your power and are living the narrative you've worked so hard to reclaim. This exercise lets you step into that future now, using your words to manifest your success.

Action: Fast forward one year from today. You've embraced your power and are living in a reality shaped by your dreams and determination. Write a diary entry as if it's a day in this future life, using the affirmations from Exercise 1 as your guide.

Prompt:

- What milestones have you achieved?
- What are you most proud of?
- How have your affirmations manifested in your life, guiding you toward this empowered state?

Reflection: This is more than an exercise in imagination—it's a way to embody your future success. By writing this paragraph, you're bringing your future self to life and ascending into that empowered version of yourself. Let the confidence and vision flow through your words, and don't hold back. This is your future, made real by your pen.

Exercise 4: Visualizing Victory – Crafting Your Triumph

Description: Freedom Dreaming is about imagining the future you want to live in, and this exercise pushes you to emotionally and mentally step into the moment when you achieve a significant goal.

Action: Choose a goal, dream, or vision you've been holding onto. Write it at the top of the page. Now, visualize the moment when you achieve that dream. Capture every detail—the setting, the emotions, the people around you, and how it feels to stand in your power having achieved this goal.

Prompt:

- How does it feel to accomplish this dream?
- Who is celebrating with you?
- What do you hear, see, smell, and touch in that moment?
- How have you transformed along the way?

Reflection: This goes beyond daydreaming by embodying your success. You're taking the abstract idea of your dream and anchoring it in your reality. As you visualize and write down this victory, you're rewiring your brain to believe that this achievement is not just possible—it's inevitable. Feel it deeply. Own it. You're already on your way.

Exercise 5: Legacy Letters – Writing Your Impact

Description: This exercise invites you to think about the legacy you want to leave behind—the impact of your story on the world. It lets you recognize the power of your words to inspire, uplift, and empower future generations.

Action: Write a letter to future generations about your journey, lessons, and the importance of believing in oneself. Let this letter reflect the growth and empowerment you've experienced on this journey and a roadmap for others to follow.

Prompt:

- What wisdom do you want to pass on to those who will come after you?
- How did you ensure your story was yours, untarnished by external doubts or negativity?
- What impact have you made on the world, and how can future generations continue your legacy of empowerment?

Reflection: This is your chance to solidify your growth and acknowledge the power you've harnessed. By writing this letter, you recognize that your story doesn't end with you—it leaves a ripple effect. You're lighting the path for others to step into their truth, just as you've done. This letter is your legacy, penned with conviction, resilience, and power.

Final Thoughts

You are the architect of your destiny. No one else can build the life you want for you. You have the power, the tools, and the courage to create the future you dream of.

Take this moment. Feel that power within you. You've come so far, and you're just getting started.

Chapter 5

Voice of the Soul

Connect deeply with your inner voice, using writing to express your most authentic self.

Close your eyes for a moment. Feel the steady rhythm of your heart, the pulse that has carried you through every challenge, every victory, every step of this journey; slowly release the tension in your shoulders, fall away, and let yourself be here—fully present, completely open. You've reached a pivotal moment in your path, a space where the noise of the outside world begins to fade, and what's left is the voice that has been with you all along—the voice of your soul. This is your time to listen, to tune into the truths you've been carrying deep inside. Up until now, you've been exploring beneath the surface of doubt, fear, and self-criticism. But now? It's time to unlock what's been quietly waiting within you. The whispers of your soul—the inner truths that have been stifled by external noise and internal hesitation—are ready to be heard. In Chapter 4, we addressed Empowerment; in this chapter, Voice of the Soul, it is time to let the world hear the empowering voice you have developed. You are ready to tune in, get quiet enough to listen, and allow your words to flow from the deepest, most genuine part of yourself.

Your soul holds the blueprint of your life's unique expression. The more you listen, the more you'll realize that this isn't just your voice—it's the voice of your ancestors, your community, and your lived experience. When you honor that voice, something shifts. Writing becomes less of a task and more of a revelation. You're not "creating" so much as revealing what's already there, waiting to be released.

The Quiet Power of Listening

We live in a world that never stops. Notifications, headlines, opinions, and endless noise surround us, making it easy to lose track of our own inner thoughts. But your soul doesn't compete with this chaos—it speaks quietly beneath it all, waiting for you to slow down and create the stillness needed to hear it clearly.

When was the last time you truly listened to yourself? Not the constant mental chatter or the demands of your to-do list, but the deeper, quieter part of you—the part that knows your deepest needs, your hidden dreams, and even your unspoken fears. This is where your untold stories live, where the truths you've been hesitant to acknowledge reside.

Listening to yourself requires trust. Trust that what arises, whether it brings comfort or discomfort, deserves your attention. Your inner voice has been with you all along, offering gentle guidance, even when you weren't fully aware of it. But to hear it, you must quiet the noise around you and within.

The next time you sit down to write, **close your eyes, take a deep breath, and ask yourself: What is the most honest thing I can say right now?** Then, write without stopping, without editing, and without judgment. Let the truth flow, even if it feels messy or raw. What emerges may surprise you—often, it's exactly what you've needed to hear all along.

By truly listening, you tap into more than just your thoughts—you unlock the core truths that have been waiting to be expressed.

Soul Work and the Process of Writing

Writing from the soul is about laying your truth bare on the page, even when that truth feels jumbled or imperfect, and not obsessing about crafting perfect sentences or obsessing over grammar. It's digging deep and trusting that what you uncover—no matter how untidy—matters.

This kind of writing calls for bravery. It doesn't allow for the usual glossing over uncomfortable feelings. It invites you to sit with the vulnerable, the flawed, the beautiful, and the not-so-beautiful aspects of yourself. But something freeing happens when you write this way. You begin to let go of the judgments and expectations that once confined you. The more you open yourself to this, the more naturally your words will come—not through force, but because you've removed the barriers that held them back.

Those words have always been within you, waiting. Your task isn't to force them out but to clear away the fears and doubts that have kept them locked away. When you do, writing becomes a natural flow—an authentic expression of who you are.

Tapping Into the Power of Ancestral Stories

Your voice carries the reverberations of generations. Whether you realize it or not, your soul is a vessel for ancestral stories. You are the continuation of a long line of resilience, wisdom, and survival. The struggles, victories, and lessons of your ancestors live within you, waiting to be honored and shared.

Gloria Anzaldúa, in her transformative work Borderlands/La Frontera, understood this on a cellular level. She wrote from a place where cultures, identities, and histories intersect, from the nepantla—the in-between space where borders dissolve and new understandings emerge. Anzaldúa believed that our souls carry the wounds and resilience of those who came before us. When we write—when we create—we are not just expressing our own voice but the voices of our people. For Anzaldúa, this wasn't just intellectual—it was soul work. She wrote to unearth and heal the collective trauma of her ancestors while celebrating their wisdom and joy.

Like Anzaldúa, you, too, are a vessel for ancestral stories. Even if you've never met the people who carried them, their experiences flow through you. Their struggles, triumphs, and lessons are embedded in your soul, waiting to be told. When you listen to the wisdom of your lineage, your writing becomes more than a personal reflection—it becomes a continuation of a larger narrative. You write not just for yourself but for your ancestors, your community, and the generations yet to come.

Honoring the Truth in Your Words

Writing from the soul isn't about getting it "right." It's about getting it real. It's about trusting that what you have to say matters, no matter how imperfect it may seem. Your words are a reflection of your journey, your truths, and your inner wisdom. And your voice? It carries power—both for you and for those who need to hear it.

When you write from this place of authenticity, the process becomes less about pleasing others or seeking validation. It becomes a journey of self-discovery and healing. Your writing will flow, not because you're trying to meet external standards but because you're expressing what's most true for you.

Here's where the soul work comes in. It's not always easy to sit with the rawness of your truth. It can be chaotic and emotional. But that's where the magic happens. In the rawness, in the vulnerability, in the courage to face yourself fully—that's where transformation lies. This is where your words gain the power to inspire, heal, and connect with others.

Making Space for Soul Work

Clearing the way for soul work in your life requires intention. It doesn't happen by accident, especially in a world that constantly pulls your attention away from your inner self. You have to be deliberate about carving out time to listen deeply to the voice within.

Mindfulness is one of the simplest ways to make space for the soul to work. Take a few minutes each day to breathe, to sit in stillness, and to listen. Ask yourself: What is my soul trying to tell me today? The answers might not come right away, but if you make space for them, they will come.

You might also find that your soul speaks more clearly when you're in nature. The stillness of the natural world has a way of quieting the noise of daily life and bringing you back to yourself. Whether you go for a walk, sit by a river, or stand barefoot on the earth, let nature guide you back to your own stillness.

The more you make space for your soul to speak, the easier it becomes to hear its voice. And when you listen, the process of writing shifts. It's no longer about effort—it's about flow. The words will come, not because you're forcing them but because they've been waiting to be released.

Writing as a Spiritual Practice

When you approach writing as soul work, it becomes a spiritual practice. Writing is no longer just a tool for expression—it becomes a way to connect with your higher self. Each word you write is an act of communion with the deepest parts of who you are.

Think of writing as a form of meditation. Just as meditation requires stillness and focus, writing from the soul requires you to be present. It asks you to let go of distractions, quiet your mind, and allow the words to flow from a place of truth. The more you practice, the more natural it becomes.

Writing can become your sacred space—a place you return to again and again to listen, reflect, and connect with your inner wisdom. This is where you honor the voice of your soul and the stories it carries, not just for yourself but a way of paying homage to your ancestors and gifting the generations to come. As you begin to channel the wisdom of your future self, the next step is to trust in the process—trust in the flow that guides you.

Trusting the Flow

Listening to the voice of your soul is also an act of trust. It's about trusting that your words—whether they come easily or with difficulty—carry weight. It's about trusting that your truth matters and that the process of writing when it comes from the soul, will guide you exactly where you need to go.

So, take another deep breath. Trust that your soul knows the way. Trust that when you create the space to listen, the words will come. And trust that those words—your words—carry the power to heal, inspire, and transform.

Your soul has been waiting for this moment. Let it speak.

The soul always knows
what to do to heal itself.
The challenge is to
silence the mind

— CAROLINE MYSS

Outcomes for Chapter 5

By the end of this chapter, you will achieve the following.

1. Tap into your authentic voice and discover the stories your soul has longed to tell.

2. Every time you write, you'll free yourself from the limitations of silence and fear. You're moving into a new realm of possibility—one where your voice is your most powerful tool.

3. You are beyond dreaming. You're speaking, writing, and acting from a place of deep empowerment, knowing that your voice can change you—and the world around you.

Overall Objective: To help you explore your soul's resonance and uncover the raw essence of your voice. This chapter is designed to guide you in peeling back societal layers, connecting with ancestral wisdom, and embracing unfiltered authenticity. These activities will help you shift from introspection to bold, fearless expression, aligning your writing with the rhythm of your soul and declaring your purpose.

I know we've just gotten into some deep stuff, and that's important. But let's not forget to keep it light when we need to. Finding your voice doesn't have to be some grand, dramatic moment where the clouds part and the angels sing. Sometimes it's messy. Sometimes, it's writing a sentence that makes no sense but makes you giggle.

If you're sitting there thinking, "Am I really ready for this?" know: You don't need to be ready. You just need to start. Take a break if you need it. Laugh at the process. Then, come back to the page with all the imperfections, quirks, and beauty that make your voice uniquely yours.

Exercise 1: Soulful Echoes Journaling

Objective: Connect with your innermost thoughts, emotions, and stories and uncover the truth waiting to be expressed.

Activity: Dedicate 20 minutes daily to journaling, focusing on listening to your soul. Use prompts such as:

- "Today, my soul feels…"
- "The unspoken words within me are…"
- "What my heart needs me to know right now is…"

The key is to let your pen flow without hesitation or self-censorship. Don't worry about grammar, structure, or making sense. This exercise is about opening a direct channel between your soul and the page. Read over your entries at the end of each week and highlight any recurring themes, emotions, or insights. These are the reverberations of your true voice, the foundation of your writing's authenticity and power.

Reflection: This exercise reinforces the chapter's message of listening to your voice and its connection to more profound truths. By reflecting weekly, you actively witness the emergence of your authentic self, providing real-time feedback on your growth.

Exercise 2: The Echo Chamber

Objective: To separate your authentic voice from external influences, allowing you to reclaim your true sound.

Activity: Choose a topic that sparks your passion—something that truly lights you up. Write a short piece on it, letting your thoughts flow naturally and without overthinking. When finished, rewrite it twice:

1. Version 1: Write it to please a specific audience (e.g., a formal publication, a group of friends, or someone whose approval you seek).

2. Version 2: Write it as if no one would ever read it—write purely for yourself, with zero judgment, inhibition, or concern for approval.

Now, compare the two rewrites. What changes when you're writing for others? What parts of your authentic voice are stripped away when you're performing for approval? In the unfiltered version, you will find the raw essence of your voice. Highlight those moments where your soul speaks—this is the voice of your freedom.

Reflection: This exercise deepens the chapter's exploration of liberation through self-expression, allowing you to actively confront and dismantle external pressures that limit your voice. It encourages conscious awareness of how your voice changes when shaped by others versus when it's entirely your own.

Exercise 3: The Soundtrack of Your Soul

Objective: To explore the connection between music and writing, using rhythm, tone, and emotion to amplify your voice.

Activity: Select a piece of music that deeply resonates with your current mood. It could be soothing, energizing, or emotionally charged—whatever mirrors your state of mind. Listen to the music, close your eyes, and be fully present with it. After a few minutes, begin freewriting. Let the music guide your pen. Don't worry about coherence; let the rhythm and emotion of the music flow into your words.

Afterward, read over your writing and reflect on how the music influenced your thoughts, tone, and flow. Did the rhythm translate into the structure of your sentences? Did the emotion of the song shift the direction of your writing? This exercise teaches you to sync your internal rhythm with your voice, creating harmony between your feelings and words.

Reflection: This exercise connects deeply with freedom dreaming, allowing your internal and external environments to merge creatively. It encourages you to trust your instincts and emotions as powerful elements of your authentic voice.

Exercise 4: Ancestral Conversations

Objective: To connect with your cultural or ancestral roots, weaving their stories and wisdom into your writing.

Activity: Take time to reflect on your ancestry, whether it's your direct family, cultural heritage, or historical figures who resonate with you. Ask yourself:

- What stories have been passed down to me?
- How do the experiences of my ancestors shape my voice today?
- What wisdom do they carry that I can honor through my writing?

Now, write a letter to one of your ancestors (whether known or unknown) and express how their journey influences your own. Then, write a response from them—offer yourself wisdom, encouragement, or guidance from their perspective. This exercise connects you to a deeper generational strength, adding a rich, layered texture to your writing.

Reflection: This exercise beautifully aligns with amplifying the freedom dream by reminding you that your voice is not just your own—it's part of a larger legacy. It strengthens your connection to personal and collective narratives, enriching the emotional depth of your writing.

Exercise 5: The Voice Declaration

Objective: To craft a powerful declaration of your unique voice and its purpose in your writing journey.

Activity: Reflect on what you've uncovered so far in this chapter. With all that in mind, write your "Voice Declaration"—a personal manifesto that captures the essence of your voice and its mission. Make it bold and unapologetic. Use affirmations that will guide your writing and reinforce your belief in the power of your words.

Examples:

- "My voice is bold and unapologetic, and I will use it to tell stories that matter."
- "I write for those whose voices have been silenced, and I amplify truths that need to be heard."
- "Every word I write brings me closer to the freedom my soul seeks."

This declaration is your guiding star. Keep it close—taped to your desk, in your journal, or as a daily mantra to remind you of the power and purpose behind your writing.

Reflection: The Voice Declaration aligns with owning and celebrating your authentic voice. It clearly affirms your journey and commitment to continue dreaming and writing freely.

Final Thoughts

You've come a long way. You've faced your doubts and inner critic, and now you stand at the threshold of your voice. This is your moment. Every word you write is a declaration: I am here. I matter. My story matters. The world is ready to listen, but most importantly, you're ready to speak.

As you move through these exercises, keep returning to the same question: What does my soul want to say today? Let that be your compass, and let your voice rise.

Our next chapter promises even more revelations. Keep tuning in and exploring, and remember: your voice is a gift, and the world needs to hear it. Your voice is the revolution.

Chapter 6

Write Now Overcome Procrastination to Unleash Your Creativity

Tackle procrastination and learn strategies to engage with your writing practice consistently.

By making it to this chapter, you've already done something pretty remarkable—you've committed to understanding yourself, owning your unique voice, and progressing fully into your creative potential. That's no small feat! But now, we've hit a bump in the road, something every writer—heck, every human—faces at some point: procrastination. As we discussed in Chapter 1, where Freedom Dreaming helps us envision our future, procrastination often stands in the way of fully realizing that vision.

Procrastination is that little voice in your head that says, "Oh, I'll write later. I just need to organize my pens first," or, "I'll get started once everything feels *perfect*—after I clean the house, scroll through Instagram, and maybe reorganize the spice rack." It's sneaky. Procrastination shows up in its pajamas, ready to make you believe that over-delaying is somehow productive. It's persistent, a master of excuses, and before you know it, the day's gone, and your writing hasn't even had a chance to stretch its legs.

Procrastination, this sneaky bugger, makes you believe that you are lazy or lack discipline. It's way more nuanced than that, and instead of pushing it away or pretending it doesn't exist, let's get to know it. If we can understand where procrastination comes from, we can start outsmarting it. Together, we'll break it down, explore why it keeps coming over unannounced, and—most importantly—find ways to kick it out for good (or at least keep it from hogging all the snacks). So, let's dig in and arm ourselves with the tools to push past procrastination and get to what matters—*your writing*.

Procrastination: The Real Story

All right, let's get one thing straight and do away with the myth once and for all - procrastination isn't a character flaw, no matter what that little voice in your head might be whispering. If you've ever thought, "Why can't I just sit down and *do the thing*?" you're not alone. The truth is that procrastination is much more human and complicated than we often give it credit for.

Think of procrastination as an overly cautious friend who's constantly afraid you'll trip over your shoelaces if you walk too fast. It's trying to protect you from failure, the anxiety of starting something big, or even the fear of succeeding. Sometimes, the sheer size of our creative dreams can feel so massive that our brains go, *"Nope, too much!"* and rather than risk not measuring up, we hit the pause button. Sound familiar?

In fact, research from Dr. Timothy Pychyl, a leading scholar on procrastination, suggests that procrastination is more about emotional regulation than time management. It's a way we cope with the negative emotions associated with starting or completing tasks, like anxiety or self-doubt. Understanding procrastination helps us break free from it. Instead of brushing it off or battling it like an enemy, let's get curious about it. What if we could understand where procrastination comes from and, even better, outsmart it? Let's break it down and give you the tools to push past it and reclaim your creative flow.

Psychologists identify these mental patterns as *cognitive distortions*. These are thought patterns that skew our perception of reality in ways that aren't helpful. Two of the big culprits in procrastination are *all-or-nothing thinking* and *catastrophizing*.

- *All-or-nothing thinking* goes like this: *"If it's not perfect, why bother?"* You set such a high bar for yourself that the mere thought of not reaching it paralyzes you.
- *Catastrophizing* is that fun little trick where your brain takes one potential setback and turns it into an epic disaster. It's the *"If I don't nail this, everything will fall apart"* type of thinking that makes us want to avoid even starting.

These thought patterns, while totally normal, can fuel our procrastination. They trigger our fears and make us want to avoid the task altogether. But here's the good news: once we recognize these sneaky thought distortions for what they are, we can begin to dismantle them. It's like finding the hidden traps in a video game—once you know where they are, you can dodge them.

Let's explore some of the most common roots of procrastination and how they might be creeping into your writing life. You're not alone in this, and we can totally outsmart it together.

1. Fear of Imperfection

At the heart of procrastination often lies fear—specifically, the fear of not being perfect. You may be holding yourself to impossibly high standards, terrified that what you create won't live up to your own expectations or the expectations of others. When you pour your heart and soul into your work, the pressure to get it *just right* can be paralyzing. So, instead of moving forward, we stall. We wait for the "perfect" moment, the "perfect" idea, or the "perfect" conditions. Spoiler alert: there is no perfect. What's important is starting, even when it's disorganized.

2. Overwhelm by the Big Picture

Does your writing feel like standing at the foot of a mountain, staring up at the seemingly endless climb ahead? The sheer magnitude of your dreams can be exhilarating—but also terrifying. Looking at the journey ahead, it's easy to feel overwhelmed. You start thinking about everything you want to write, all the emotions you want to capture, and it feels like too much. Instead of taking one step, you freeze.

The trick? Break it down. Focus on the next word, the next sentence, the next paragraph. The mountain will still be there, but you can only climb it one step at a time.

3. Distractions and External Demands

Life is full of distractions. Whether it's work, social obligations, or even the lure of scrolling through social media, countless things are competing for your attention. And sometimes, these distractions feel like the perfect excuse to put off writing. After all, there's always tomorrow, right?

Distractions will always exist. The key is learning to navigate them without losing sight of what's important to *you*. Writing doesn't demand hours of uninterrupted time—it demands commitment, even if it's just 10 minutes a day. Consistency, not perfection, is what builds habits.

4. A Disconnected "Why"

Why did you start writing in the first place? Was it to tell a story that's been burning inside you? To process your thoughts and emotions? To connect with others or leave a lasting impact? Whatever your "why" is, it's your driving force. But that "why" can get lost in the shuffle of life's demands and distractions over time.

When you lose touch with your "why," procrastination creeps in. Writing feels more like a chore than a calling. This chapter is about reconnecting with that original spark, reigniting your passion, and using it to fuel your writing, no matter your obstacles.

Strategies for Overcoming Procrastination

Now that we've identified some of the roots of procrastination let's talk about how to overcome it. These strategies avoid forcing yourself to be productive and instead shift your mindset to get out of your own way.

1. Start Small, But Start

Forget the idea that you need hours of free time to get any real writing done. Start with just five or ten minutes a day. Set a timer, sit down, and write without judgment. When the timer goes off, stop. You'll be surprised at how much you can accomplish in short bursts, and you'll start building traction. The more you show up, even in small ways, the easier it becomes.

2. Break Down the Mountain

Remember that overwhelming feeling of staring at the big picture? Break it down. Instead of thinking about the entire project, focus on one tiny part. Write one paragraph or even one sentence. Take it step by step, and soon, you'll find yourself making progress without feeling weighed down by the enormity of the task.

3. Create a Distraction-Free Space

Identify your biggest distractions and create a writing environment that minimizes them. Maybe that means turning off your phone, finding a quiet corner, or setting boundaries with the people around you. Your writing time is sacred—treat it as such. Even if it's just 15 minutes, permit yourself to be fully present in those moments.

4. Reconnect with Your "Why"

When you feel stuck or unmotivated, take a moment to remember *why* you started writing in the first place. Write it down. Pin it somewhere you can see every day. Your "why" is your anchor—it will keep you going when procrastination tries to derail you. Every time you sit down to write, remind yourself that your words matter, your story matters, and the world needs to hear your voice.

5. Progress Over Perfection

This is a big one. Instead of trying to get it right the first time, embrace the messy, imperfect writing process. Your first draft doesn't need to be brilliant—it just needs to exist. You can always revise and polish it later. For now, focus on getting the words out. It's better to have something to improve than nothing at all.

I have come to believe over and over again that what is most important to me must be spoken, made verbal and shared, even at the risk of having it bruised or misunderstood.

— AUDRE LORDE

Outcomes for Chapter 6

By the end of this chapter, you will:

1. Understand the real reasons behind your procrastination, like fear of failure or feeling overwhelmed, and recognize that it's manageable, not a personal flaw.
2. Learn to let go of perfectionism, focus on progress over perfection, and embrace the messy, imperfect writing process.
3. Be equipped with practical tools to stay on track, such as breaking tasks into small steps, starting with short writing bursts, and minimizing distractions.
4. Reconnect with your deeper reason for writing, using your "why" as motivation to push past procrastination.
5. Gain confidence to take consistent, manageable steps in your writing, building on the progress and unlocking your full creative potential.

Overall Objective: To help you confront the root causes of procrastination and perfectionism. This chapter offers practical tools to break down overwhelming tasks, reframe limiting thoughts, and build momentum in your writing. These activities are designed to create a distraction-free environment, foster accountability, and help you focus on progress over perfection, allowing your voice to thrive with confidence and consistency.

Exercise 1: The "Why Not Now?" Reflection

Objective: To uncover the real reasons behind your procrastination and understand what's holding you back.

Activity: Set a timer for 10 minutes and write an honest answer to this question: "Why am I avoiding this task right now?" Don't filter yourself. Write freely and let any feelings, thoughts, or excuses pour out.

▸ Are you afraid of failing?

▸ Do you feel overwhelmed by how much there is to do?

▸ Are you worried it won't turn out the way you imagine?

Once the 10 minutes are up, read through what you've written. Highlight any recurring fears or thoughts. These are the underlying roots of your procrastination. Knowing what's driving the avoidance is the first step toward tackling it.

Exercise 2: Break the All-or-Nothing Trap

Objective: To challenge all-or-nothing thinking and break tasks into smaller, manageable pieces.

Activity: Take a writing project (or any task) you've been putting off because it feels too big or overwhelming. Now, break it down into the smallest steps possible. We're talking tiny steps.

For example, if you're working on a book:

- Instead of thinking, "I need to write a chapter," think, "I'll write the first sentence of the chapter."
- Instead of thinking, "I need to outline the entire plot," think, "I'll brainstorm three plot ideas today."

The Goal: Complete one tiny step each day. When you've done that, celebrate it. Acknowledge that progress is progress, no matter how small.

Exercise 3: The 5-Minute Jumpstart

Objective: To trick your brain into starting a task by lowering the stakes and reducing anxiety.

Activity: The next time you feel procrastination creeping in, commit to working on your task for just five minutes. Set a timer and dive in. Once the five minutes are up, you're free to stop. But here's the catch— you'll usually want to keep going once you've started.

Why This Works: Setting such a short, manageable time frame reduces the pressure of the task. The hardest part of writing (or any project) is often just getting started. The 5-minute jumpstart removes the mental roadblocks by permitting you to stop after a short amount of time.

Exercise 4: Overcoming Catastrophizing with Reframing

Objective: To challenge catastrophic thinking and reframe fears in a more productive, realistic way.

Activity: The next time you catch yourself thinking something like, "If I fail at this, everything will fall apart," take a moment to reframe that thought. Ask yourself:

- What's the worst that could happen if this doesn't go perfectly?
- Will it indeed be a disaster, or am I exaggerating the outcome?
- What's a more realistic outcome?
- What can I do to make the situation more manageable?

Write out both your catastrophic thought and your reframed, more realistic version. By actively reframing these thoughts, you'll begin to see how much power they lose when exposed to logic and reason.

Exercise 5: Reconnect with Your "Why"

Objective: To reignite your motivation and clarify your reasons for starting the project in the first place.

Activity: Write down your "why." Why are you writing? Why is this project important to you? Be honest with yourself and dig deep into what's driving you—personal growth, a desire to tell your story, to challenge yourself, etc.

Prompt:

- Why did I start this project?
- What do I hope to accomplish through my writing?
- How will I feel once I've completed it?

Once you've written down your reasons, post them somewhere visible. Anytime procrastination starts to creep in, revisit your "why." Let it remind you of your purpose and reignite your passion.

Exercise 6: Create a Distraction-Free Zone

Objective: To minimize external distractions and create a focused writing environment.

Activity: Identify your biggest distractions. Is it your phone? The internet? Noise around you? Set up a writing space where these distractions are minimized. Try these strategies:

▸ Set your phone to Do Not Disturb or put it in another room.

▸ Use an app or browser extension that blocks distracting websites during your writing time (e.g., StayFocusd or Freedom).

▸ Choose a specific time each day when distractions are minimal, and commit to writing during that time.

The Goal: Create a 20-minute distraction-free writing block each day. You'll be amazed at how much you can accomplish when your focus is undisturbed.

Exercise 7: Progress Over Perfection Mantra

Objective: To overcome perfectionism by focusing on making progress, not achieving flawless results.

Activity: Write out the following mantra and keep it nearby as a reminder whenever you sit down to write: "Progress over perfection. I give myself permission to create without judgment. My first draft doesn't need to be perfect—it just needs to exist."

Whenever you catch yourself holding back because it's "not good enough," read this mantra out loud. Remind yourself that no one ever wrote a perfect first draft. The goal is to keep moving forward, even if it's messy.

Exercise 8: Accountability Partner Check-In

Objective: To create accountability and motivation through a trusted partner.

Activity: Find an accountability partner—someone who will check in with you regularly about your writing progress. It could be a fellow writer, a friend, or a family member. Set up weekly check-ins to share what you've accomplished, whether it's a few paragraphs or an outline of your ideas.

What If Your Accountability Partner Doesn't Show Up? Sometimes, life happens, and your partner may not be able to follow through consistently. If that happens:

1. Become Your Own Accountability Partner: If your partner misses a check-in, don't let that stop your progress. Set a reminder for yourself to check in with your own goals. Reflect on your achievements and challenges for the week. Write down your progress, even if no one else is asking for it.
2. Create a Backup Plan: Have a secondary plan in place, such as joining a writer's group or using an accountability app that tracks your writing habits. This ensures you have another layer of support.
3. Be Honest and Reassess: If your partner consistently doesn't show up, have an honest conversation about whether this arrangement is still helpful for both of you. You may need to find a new partner who is more aligned with your goals and schedule.

Final Thoughts

You've moved past procrastination by embracing action. You've realized that every time you sit down to write, you are creating forward movement. By now, you've shifted from hesitating to actively creating. Keep this up. The more you write, the more empowered you become. The next step is harnessing this energy and turning your dreams into tangible results.

So grab your pen, your journal, and let's write now.

Chapter 7

Bracing for Setbacks

Illuminate your journey with insights and techniques to enhance your creative writing process.

In Chapter 5, we faced down the relentless voice of the internal critic—the one that insists we aren't good enough, smart enough, or creative enough. In Chapter 6, we confronted procrastination head-on, peeling back the layers of resistance that keep us from doing the work we know we're capable of. But here's the truth: these are not the only challenges you will face. Setbacks come in many forms, and they're an inevitable part of the journey.

No matter how prepared you feel, setbacks will arise. They may be external—unexpected disruptions, rejections, or criticism. Or they may emerge from within—self-doubt returning just when you thought you'd conquered it, old fears resurfacing in moments of vulnerability. Even though when they occur, remember that setbacks aren't signs of failure; they can be proof you're on a path worth pursuing. Every great creator, thinker, and writer has faced them. The key is learning how to brace for them, building the internal resilience required to keep moving forward, even when things don't go as planned.

Elizabeth Gilbert reminds us in *Big Magic* that fear and uncertainty are woven into the creative process. "You can measure your worth by your dedication to your path, not by your successes or failures," she says. In other words, setbacks are not the enemy—they are part of the process. They challenge your commitment and offer an opportunity to grow, strengthen your resolve, and show up again, no matter how many times you stumble.

In this chapter, we'll learn how to brace for setbacks and build the muscle to face these moments together so that no matter what challenges arise, you can keep moving forward with clarity and purpose.

So, let's get comfy with the idea that things won't always go according to our meticulously crafted plans. Let's accept that sometimes the universe likes to toss a banana peel right in our path—not to make us fall, but to see if we can turn it into a comedic slide, into something even better. Let's figure out when to wrap ourselves in a blanket of grace and when to give ourselves that much-needed nudge (or firm kick in the pants). Both are essential ingredients in this wild, wonderful journey we're on together.

Setbacks: The Detours on Your Road Trip

Imagine you're on a road trip. You've mapped out your route, planned your stops, and you're cruising along, enjoying the scenery. Then, suddenly, you hit a detour. The road is blocked, and now you're forced to take a winding, unfamiliar route that adds extra miles to your journey. Frustrating, right? I know it is, but while they're inconvenient and unexpected, they often lead you to places you wouldn't have discovered otherwise—hidden gems, scenic overlooks, or new experiences you never planned for.

That's what setbacks are. They're the unexpected detours in your journey. They slow you down, take you off course, and force you to rethink your route. But if you lean into them, they often reveal something important— a new skill, a lesson in resilience, or a different perspective you wouldn't have gained if everything had gone smoothly. Just like a road trip, the journey isn't about getting from point A to point B without any bumps. It's about how you adapt to the unexpected turns and the growth that happens along the way.

So, next time you face a setback, think of it as a detour—not an obstacle. It may not be the route you planned, but it's still part of the journey, and it might just take you somewhere even better than you expected.

Why Setbacks Happen (And Why They Can Be Good for You)

Psychological research shows that setbacks can actually be valuable opportunities for growth. According to **Carol Dweck**, a professor of psychology at Stanford University and a pioneer in the study of *mindset*, setbacks are crucial in fostering a *growth mindset*. A growth mindset is the belief that abilities and intelligence can be developed through dedication and hard work. Dweck's research highlights that people who view challenges and setbacks as opportunities to learn and develop are more likely to persist in the face of adversity, ultimately leading to greater long-term success.

What Dweck's research reveals is that setbacks are not indicators of failure—they are essential parts of progress. People with a growth mindset recognize that every setback is a push toward mastery, resilience, and creative problem-solving. They understand that success doesn't come from avoiding obstacles but from learning how to overcome them. **Thomas Edison** famously remarked, *"I have not failed. I've just found 10,000 ways that won't work."* Each of those "failures" brought him closer to success precisely because he viewed setbacks as learning opportunities, not as reflections of his inadequacy.

When we face a setback, we have a choice: we can either see it as evidence that we're not good enough, or we can approach it as an invitation to strengthen our resilience and expand our problem-solving abilities. Setbacks, while often frustrating, push us to innovate and test our limits. They force us to dig deeper, get creative, and develop solutions that we might never have considered if everything had gone according to plan.

This challenge-response mechanism builds mental fortitude, a trait that's essential for navigating life's unpredictabilities. Every time you encounter a setback, you're not just finding a way around a temporary obstacle— you're training yourself for future challenges. With each setback you face and overcome, your capacity for perseverance grows. Research published in the **Journal of Personality and Social Psychology** suggests that individuals who experience and overcome challenges become more emotionally resilient and are better equipped to handle future stressors.

Setbacks also have a way of revealing hidden strengths. It's only when you're forced to problem-solve and adapt that you realize your true capabilities. You might discover that you're more resourceful than you thought or that you have untapped reserves of determination. Setbacks challenge you to think differently, to question old approaches, and to step outside of your comfort zone—all of which contribute to long-term growth and success.

Consider some of the greats.

- ▸ **J.K. Rowling**: She didn't just waltz into a publishing house and walk out with a deal for *Harry Potter*. Her manuscript was rejected a dozen times. Instead of seeing those rejections as indicating that her writing wasn't good enough, she viewed them as part of the journey. Her perseverance transformed those setbacks into a building block for something greater than she could have imagined.
- ▸ **Elizabeth Gilbert**: The author of *Eat, Pray, Love* faced countless rejections before her breakout hit. She's been open about the fact that failure is part of the writer's life—and how embracing that failure led her to a deeper, richer relationship with her craft.

Here's why setbacks can be *good* for you:

1. **They Strengthen Your Grit** – Setbacks give you the opportunity to strengthen your grit. Each time you encounter a challenge and push through it, you're proving to yourself that you can endure and navigate difficult times.

2. **They Sharpen Your Skills** - Hitting a wall makes you more resourceful. Suddenly, you're not just relying on your go-to techniques. You have to think differently, maybe even step outside your comfort zone. And that is where growth happens.

3. **They Keep You Humble (in a Good Way)** - Sometimes, we need a reminder that we don't have it all figured out, and that's okay. Setbacks keep us grounded and help us appreciate the journey rather than just focusing on the destination.

4. **They Force You to Ask, "Why?"** - Often, setbacks are a wake-up call. They make you pause and reconsider: *Why am I doing this? What's my real motivation?* If you've lost sight of your purpose, a setback will shine a spotlight on that and give you a chance to reconnect with your "why."

Embracing Setbacks: Finding the Lessons

We've established that setbacks are useful, but that doesn't mean they don't suck in the moment. It's hard to see the silver lining when you're staring at a blank screen or feeling like your latest draft is a dumpster fire. But the magic happens in those frustrating moments where valuable lessons wait to be learned.

The key is *not to resist* them. When a setback shows up, don't throw up your hands and declare defeat. Instead, ask yourself:

- *What is this trying to teach me?*
- *Is there something I need to adjust in my approach?*
- *Am I clinging too tightly to a particular outcome?*

And sometimes the lesson is simply this: messing up is okay. It's okay to take a break, regroup, and return stronger. Setbacks aren't signs that you're failing; they're part of the learning process. After all, the only way to avoid setbacks is not to try at all—and we both know you're not about that life.

Giving Yourself Grace (When You Need It)

Sometimes, after hitting a wall, what you need is a little compassion—*from yourself.* We can be our own worst critics, but you're allowed not to have it all together. You're allowed off days. You're allowed to take breaks without feeling guilty about it.

So, how do you know when to give yourself grace? Here are a few signs:

- You're completely burnt out, both creatively and emotionally.
- Your inner critic has taken over, and no amount of pep talks silences it.

- You've been pushing yourself so hard that the joy has been sucked out of the process.

When you find yourself in this space, it's time to step back, take a breath, and permit yourself to rest. Not every moment has to be about pushing forward. Sometimes, the best thing you can do is recharge.

Knowing When to Give Yourself a Kick in the Butt

On the flip side, there are moments when what you need isn't rest but a swift kick in the pants. Sometimes, we hide behind "taking a break" when what we're really doing is avoiding the hard work. If you've been "resting" for weeks but haven't made a plan to get back on track, it might be time to give yourself a nudge. (Okay, more like a shove.)

Ask yourself:

- Am I avoiding something difficult because it scares me?
- Have I been using rest as an excuse to procrastinate?
- Is it time to just sit down and do the work?

There's a balance here—grace when you're genuinely overwhelmed and tough love when you're avoiding the next step. And yes, sometimes it's hard to tell the difference. But that's part of the journey, too.

The wound is the place where the light enters you.

— RUMI

Outcomes for Chapter 7

By the end of this chapter, you will:

1. Redefine and view setbacks as natural and essential for growth rather than failures.
2. Build mental and emotional toughness to face challenges and keep moving forward.
3. Adapt and embrace flexibility in plans, allowing creativity to flourish even when things don't go as expected.
4. Balance grace and accountability by learning when to show self-compassion and when to push forward with determination.
5. Develop strategies for reigniting motivation and turning challenges into opportunities for progress.

Overall Objective: To help you confront, address, and overcome setbacks in a way that turns them into opportunities for growth rather than stumbling blocks. These activities are designed to help you reflect, learn, and move forward with resilience and purpose.

Exercise 1: The Setback Autopsy

Objective: To reflect on a past setback, understand its root cause, and extract the lesson.

Activity: Think about a recent setback (in writing or life) that left you feeling stuck or frustrated. Take 10-15 minutes to write about it, addressing the following prompts:

- What was the setback?
- How did it make you feel in the moment?
- What were the immediate thoughts and emotions that surfaced? (Were you angry, sad, or did you want to quit?)
- What do you think caused the setback? (Was it a lack of preparation, external circumstances, fear?)
- What lesson did this setback teach you?
- How would you approach this situation differently next time?

By breaking down the setback into its core parts, you'll gain clarity and see it as an opportunity for growth rather than a failure. Keep this reflection somewhere accessible as a reminder of how far you've come.

Exercise 2: The Grace vs. Push Assessment

Objective: To determine whether you need to give yourself grace or a push to get back on track.

Activity: When you encounter a setback, pause and ask yourself the following questions:

- Am I genuinely exhausted, creatively drained, or emotionally overwhelmed?
  If **yes**, give yourself grace. You're human, and sometimes, the best way forward is to take a step back and recharge.
- Am I avoiding the work because I'm afraid of failure or struggling with perfectionism?
  If **yes**, give yourself a push. Sometimes, we need to move past fear and act, even if it feels uncomfortable.

Once you've identified whether you need grace or a push, write down three things you can do:

- If you need grace, write down three ways to rest or nurture yourself (take a break, spend time doing something fun, meditate, etc.).
- If you need a push, write down three small tasks to help you start again (write for 10 minutes, outline a new section, or edit just one page).

Notice that each activity is intentionally bound by a time limit—whether it's a 5-minute break, a 30-minute fun activity, or a 20-minute meditation session. The key is setting clear boundaries to avoid slipping into excessive rest or distraction. By defining the time upfront, you give yourself permission to recharge without losing momentum. This structure ensures that you stay productive, keeping rest purposeful and preventing it from stretching into procrastination. Stick to your limits, and you'll find a balance between replenishing your energy and continuing to make progress.

Exercise 3: Embrace the Detour

Objective: To change your mindset about setbacks and learn to see them as detours, not dead ends.

Activity: Grab a piece of paper or your journal and draw a path (like a map) leading to one of your creative goals. Now, imagine that along this path, there are unexpected detours. These could be writer's block, rejection, or personal life interruptions.

Next to each "detour," write down how you would handle it. For example:

- Writer's block: Take a break and try a writing prompt.
- Rejection: Seek feedback and revise, or explore a new publication.
- Life interruptions: Set smaller, manageable writing goals until things settle.

By visualizing setbacks as detours that you can plan for and navigate around, you shift your mindset from frustration to strategy. This also reinforces that no setback is permanent; it's just part of the journey.

Exercise 4: Setback Affirmations

Objective: To create positive reminders that help you stay grounded during challenging times.

Activity: Setbacks can shake your confidence, so let's work on keeping it steady. Write down three affirmations you can repeat whenever a setback hits. These phrases should resonate with your journey and remind you of your strength.

Examples:

- ▶ "Setbacks are part of my growth; I will learn and keep moving forward."
- ▶ "Every challenge makes me a better writer and a stronger person."
- ▶ "I trust my ability to overcome obstacles and achieve my goals."

Post these affirmations somewhere visible, like your writing space or phone wallpaper. Each time you encounter a roadblock, say these affirmations aloud to remind yourself that you've got this.

Exercise 5: The Next Step Strategy

Objective: To help you take action after a setback by focusing on manageable next steps.

Activity: When a setback derails your progress, determining where to pick up again can feel overwhelming. Instead of trying to fix everything at once, identify just one small step you can take to regain mojo.

Write down the answers to these prompts:

- What's the very next step I can take to move forward? (Is it writing one paragraph, seeking feedback, or brainstorming new ideas?)
- What's my time frame for completing this step? (Set a short, realistic deadline—within a day or two—to help you stay accountable.)
- How will I reward myself once I complete this step? (Maybe it's a favorite snack, a short walk, or a fun activity to celebrate your progress.)

By focusing on the next step rather than the entire journey, you make the process more manageable and less intimidating.

Exercise 6: Setback Support System

Objective: To create a network of accountability and support during times of challenge.

Activity: Identify three people who can be part of your "setback support system." These should be individuals who encourage you, offer constructive feedback, or listen when you're feeling discouraged.

Write down their names and how they can support you:

- ▶ Who can you reach out to for advice or feedback?
- ▶ Who can provide a fresh perspective when you feel stuck?
- ▶ Who can remind you of your strengths and achievements when self-doubt creeps in?

Set a goal to check in with at least one support member whenever you hit a significant setback. Sometimes, all it takes is a different viewpoint or a pep talk to get you back on track.

Exercise 7: Reconnect with Your "Why"

Objective: To remind yourself of the purpose behind your creative journey, especially when setbacks make you doubt your path.

Activity: Take a few moments to revisit why you started this journey in the first place. Write a short letter to yourself, answering the following questions:

- Why did I begin this writing project?
- What impact do I want my words to have?
- How will I feel when I achieve this goal?

Keep this letter nearby and read it whenever setbacks feel like they're derailing your progress. Reconnecting with your "why" can reignite your passion and remind you that your creative journey is worth it.

Final Thoughts

Setbacks don't define you—they prepare you. Each obstacle, rejection, or creative block is an opportunity for growth, resilience, and learning. By embracing setbacks as part of the process and using these exercises to confront and overcome them, you're building the strength and skills to navigate any challenge that comes your way.

Remember, every setback is just a setup for a comeback. So, take a deep breath, give yourself grace when needed, push yourself when required, and keep moving forward. Your writing journey, with all its twists and turns, is leading you exactly where you're meant to be.

Adaptive Strategies for Overcoming Creative Setbacks

ROADBLOCK	ADAPTIVE STRATEGIES
Fear of Imperfection	Embrace the "progress over perfection" mindset. Write your first draft freely without self-editing. Remind yourself that progress is more important than perfection.
Overwhelm from Large Projects	Break your writing project into small, manageable tasks. Set achievable deadlines for each part. Celebrate completing each step to stay motivated and encouraged.
Writer's Block	Engage in creative activities like drawing or listening to music to stimulate new ideas. Try free writing or creative prompts to break through the block.

Frequent Distractions	Identify peak productivity hours and plan writing sessions during those times. Use apps to block distractions or turn off your phone. Create a distraction-free zone.
Loss of Interest in Topic	Reconnect with the original excitement for your topic. Pivot slightly if needed to align with what currently interests you. Take breaks to reignite passion.
Negative Self-Talk	Counter self-doubt with positive affirmations. Maintain a "success journal" to record small victories and remind yourself of your progress and achievements.
Constantly Seeking Feedback	Set specific points in your writing process for seeking feedback. Trust your instincts and let your writing develop naturally before seeking external input.

Chapter 8

Authentic Resonance

Develop an authentic writing style that resonates with your experiences and beliefs.

You've already done incredible work uncovering your voice and setting the groundwork for your writing journey, but now it's time to take things up a notch. Think of this as leveling up—because this chapter is all about **authenticity**. As you craft your authentic narrative, remember the exercises from Chapter 2, where you started homing in on your unique voice, and in Chapter 4, where we talked about embracing empowerment by stripping away pretense. Now, let's build on those foundations. This chapter will help you find your authentic voice and use it to connect with your readers. We'll explore how to break free from expectations and write from the heart. When you finish, you'll feel more in tune with your unique writing style and confident in expressing aligning with the person you're meant to be.

"Authenticity" is one of those words that gets thrown around a lot these days, like it belongs on a Pinterest board or stitched onto a throw pillow. But in writing, authenticity is far from a buzzword. It's not some trendy thing you slap on a bumper sticker; it's the heartbeat of your craft. It's the secret sauce that turns good writing into something that *sticks—*

something that resonates so deeply that it feels like it's speaking straight to the soul. That's the real magic: when your truth finds its way into readers' hearts, making them feel like you've seen into their lives struggles and joys. That's the writer's dream.

We've already explored how writing authentically means tapping into your most authentic self. Now, let's focus on refining that authenticity, translating your raw emotions into deeply resonating stories. Authenticity creates a narrative that leaves an impact.

So, grab whatever fuels your creative spirit—a strong cup of coffee, a calming tea, or maybe something with a little more kick (no judgment here)—and let's get to work. Tapping into that honest, raw, unapologetic version of you is precisely what's going to make your writing stand out. It's what will have your readers nodding along, tearing up, or even laughing out loud, saying, "Yes! I *feel* that!"

This is your invitation to let go of the polished version of yourself that you think the world wants to see and embrace the beautifully imperfect truth of who you are. It's time to unlock your authentic voice, and trust me, the world is waiting to hear it.

Truth in Words: The Power of Authenticity

People can smell falsehood from a mile away. Whether in real life or on the page, there's something about phony, hollow words that don't sit right. But when someone writes or speaks from the heart, when they show you their *real* self, that's when the magic happens. That's when your words go from just sentences on a page to something that *moves* people.

Think about a time when you read something that stopped you in your tracks, a line so honest it felt like the writer knew exactly what you were going through. It was like they reached out from the page and whispered,

"I see you." That's the power of writing from an authentic place. When your truth meets the reader's heart, you create a bond far beyond the words themselves.

That's what we're here to do. To craft writing that resonates not just with you but with the people lucky enough to read it. Remember, it doesn't have to be perfect. It just has to be *real*.

Crafting Your Authentic Narrative

So, how do you get there? How do you create writing that feels so authentic it jumps off the page? It starts with you—your voice, your perspective, your life. This might sound daunting, but trust me, it's the most freeing thing you can do as a writer.

Authentic writing doesn't fit into someone else's box; it knocks that box over and says, *"No, thanks; I'll make my own."* You lean into what makes you *you*—your quirks, your unique way of seeing the world, your fears, and your dreams. You let yourself be vulnerable because vulnerability is the birthplace of connection.

Here's how we start crafting that authentic narrative:

1. Reflect on Your Experiences

Your life is full of stories that shape your voice as a writer. Think about the moments that have defined you—the highs, the lows, the in-betweens. What did you learn from those experiences? How do they influence the way you see the world?

Your experiences are like a treasure trove of material waiting to be mined. They give your writing its unique flavor, and when you bring those stories to the page, they resonate because they come from a place of truth.

2. Embrace Vulnerability

Vulnerability is hard. But it's also where the magic happens. When you write from a place of vulnerability, you open the door for others to connect with you. People don't resonate with perfection; they resonate with realness. When you share your struggles, your doubts, and your myriad of emotions, you're permitting others to feel theirs.

Think of Brené Brown, who built an entire movement around vulnerability. "Vulnerability is the birthplace of innovation, creativity, and change," she says. And she's right. Don't be afraid to let people see the human behind the words. That's where authenticity truly thrives.

3. Challenge Conformity

There's a lot of noise out there about what writing *should* be. What's "marketable," what "sells," what's "expected." But you don't have to follow those rules. The most authentic writing often breaks them.

Take risks with your work. Challenge the norms. Write in a way that feels true to you, not in a way you think will please others. When you stop worrying about fitting in and start embracing your voice, your writing becomes unmistakably yours. And that's when it starts to resonate with readers craving something real.

4. Keep Growing

Authenticity is an ongoing process. The more you write, the more you learn about yourself, and your voice will evolve. Allow yourself to grow, change, and explore new ideas and perspectives. The writer you are today might not be the writer you'll be tomorrow, and that's okay. In fact, it's great.

Stay open to learning—about yourself, your craft, and the world around you. Your authenticity will grow as you do.

Trust yourself.
Think for yourself.
Act for yourself.
Speak for yourself.
Be yourself.
Imitation is suicide.

– MARVA COLLINS

Outcomes for Chapter 8

By the end of this chapter, you will:

1. Have tapped into your authentic voice, learning to trust it as a powerful tool for storytelling and connection.
2. Embrace the strength that comes from writing vulnerably, understanding that it's the raw, unpolished parts of you that create the most profound connections.
3. Gain the confidence to break free from writing conventions and expectations, choosing instead to craft work that is true to who you are.
4. Recognize that your authentic voice is constantly evolving, and you'll commit to allowing your writing to grow as you do.

Overall Objective: To help you understand your deepest truths and fears, pushing past self-imposed filters to uncover your most authentic voice. This chapter offers exercises to foster vulnerability, encourage fearless self-expression, and deepen your connection with yourself and your readers. By embracing discomfort and writing without judgment, you'll cultivate a bold, resonant voice that strengthens both your craft and audience connection.

Exercise 1: The Mirror Moment

Objective: To reflect on your most honest truths and how they shape your voice as a writer.

Activity: Find a quiet space and stand in front of a mirror. Look yourself in the eyes and ask: "What's the truth I've been holding back in my writing?" It could be a belief, an experience, or even an emotion you haven't fully explored. Let it simmer for a moment.

Now, write for 15 minutes about this truth. Don't worry about grammar, structure, or how it sounds—just let the words flow. Imagine you're having a conversation with your truest self. The goal here is to get real with yourself on the page.

Reflection: Once you're done, look over what you've written. Ask yourself:

▸ Why have I held back from sharing this truth?
▸ How would embracing this truth change the way I write?

Exercise 2: Ditch the Filters

Objective: To write without fear of judgment or expectation, focusing purely on your most authentic voice.

Activity: Choose a topic you're passionate about, but this time, write about it as if no one else will ever read it. Imagine there are no editors, critics, or readers—just you and your thoughts. You are allowed to be raw, unkempt, and vulnerable.

Write freely for 20 minutes. Be bold. Let your voice come through without any filters. This is the you that exists when no one is watching.

Reflection: Compare this piece to your other recent work. What stands out? Does it feel more authentic? More like you? What would happen if you approached every piece of writing with this level of freedom?

Exercise 3: Embrace the Uncomfortable

Objective: To push through the fear of vulnerability by writing about a challenging or uncomfortable topic.

Activity: We all have stories or feelings we hesitate to share, whether out of fear of judgment or simply because they make us uncomfortable. Pick a subject you've been avoiding—maybe it's a difficult memory, an unpopular opinion, or a part of yourself you're reluctant to explore.

Write for 15 minutes on this topic. Embrace the discomfort. The goal isn't to create a masterpiece but to practice being vulnerable in your writing.

Reflection: After you've finished, take a deep breath and read what you've written. How does it feel? Do you sense a deeper connection with your own voice? How might this exercise shift the way you approach vulnerability in future work?

Exercise 4: Audience Connection

Objective: To understand how your authenticity can resonate with your readers by imagining their reactions and responses.

Activity: Imagine a group of readers encountering your most personal, honest writing. Visualize their faces as they read—are they nodding in agreement, tearing up, or laughing? Write down what you hope readers feel when they connect with your words.

Now, take 10 minutes to write a short piece (it could be a paragraph or a poem) that directly addresses your readers. Share something real that will make them feel understood, seen, or inspired. Speak directly to them in your voice.

Reflection: When you're done, ask yourself:

- How did it feel to write directly to an audience?
- What part of me did I reveal in this piece that might resonate with them?

Exercise 5: Reader Feedback

Objective: To gain insight into how your authentic voice resonates with others by seeking feedback from trusted readers.

Activity: Share a piece of writing that feels authentic to you with a trusted friend, writing partner, or group. Ask them for feedback on what parts of your voice stood out the most. What moments felt the most real to them? What did they connect with?

Use their feedback to understand better how your voice is being received and where you can lean in even more to your authenticity.

Reflection: After receiving feedback, reflect on what you've learned. Did your readers resonate with the parts of your writing that felt the most authentic to you? How can you continue to develop and refine your unique voice moving forward?

Final Thoughts

You've found your authentic voice, and it's a powerful one. You're no longer writing to fit expectations or mold yourself to external standards. Your words are now a true reflection of who you are. As you continue, your writing will only deepen in authenticity and impact. This is the voice that will resonate not just with you but with your readers as well.

Chapter 9

Let's Celebrate You!

Celebrate your progress and learn to appreciate the journey of writing as much as the destination.

Take a deep breath. Not one of those half-hearted breaths that barely makes it past your throat—a real, grounding breath. Now, look around—not at the world outside, but at the journey you've been on. Go ahead and give yourself a mental pat on the back (or, if you're feeling extra, a literal one). The person staring back at you from the mirror is not the same person who first opened this book. You've traveled through moments of discomfort, vulnerability, reflection, and resilience. You've shown up for yourself, even when Netflix was calling your name. And that? That deserves a standing ovation—*from you*.

You didn't just show up for the fun, easy parts. You stuck around when it felt uncomfortable, like pulling teeth just to write a sentence. You kept moving forward even when your self-doubt was screaming louder than a toddler in a candy store. And that kind of grit deserves celebrating—not as a reward for reaching some mythical finish line, but because it took courage to keep going.

We often reserve our celebrations for the "big" moments—like landing that dream job or reaching your goal weight. But the real victories?

They're the small, quiet ones. It's the morning you sat down to write, even though your brain was telling you, "Nope, not today." It's the time you fought through procrastination and kept going because something inside you whispered, *keep going.* That's where real success is built—in the effort, not the applause.

Why Celebrating Yourself Matters

Somehow, we've been conditioned to think that celebration is something we "earn" at the end of the journey. But let's be honest—that's like waiting until your birthday to eat cake all year. What's the point? If you're not celebrating along the way, you're missing the best parts of the ride. It's like going on a road trip and ignoring all the cool roadside attractions because you're too focused on getting to the destination.

And there's science to back this up. **Teresa Amabile**, a professor at Harvard Business School, developed something called the "progress principle." It basically says that recognizing and celebrating small wins is like giving your brain a high-five. Her studies show that even tiny victories trigger a rush of dopamine—the brain's happy juice. This makes you feel good (hello, dopamine) and reinforces the habits that help you keep going. In other words, you're literally wired to thrive on small wins.

So why wait for the big moments? Every little step you take matters. It's like putting together a puzzle. You don't throw the whole thing away because you only found one corner piece—you celebrate that piece like it's the Mona Lisa. Each step you take shapes you into the person you're becoming, and that deserves recognition. Don't wait until the picture is complete to appreciate the process.

Redefining Success: The Power of Small Wins

In a world that celebrates the "go big or go home" mentality, it's easy to forget what real success looks like. We're all trained to chase the applause—the book deal, the Instagram-worthy promotion, the flashy end result. But let's be real for a second: Success is born in the little moments. It's in the decision to sit down and write when you'd rather scroll mindlessly on your phone. It's in the courage to keep writing when the words feel like they're stuck in traffic.

Let's redefine success for a second. It's not the flashy "I made it" moment. Success is writing a single sentence when your creativity is taking a personal day. It's showing up even when your inner critic is whispering, *"This is terrible."* The small wins—the ones no one claps for—are the real foundation for everything else.

Did you write a sentence today? *Boom, success.* Did you avoid procrastinating on TikTok for a whole 15 minutes? *Another win.* Every effort, no matter how small, counts. Because those little efforts stack up and bring you closer to becoming the writer, creator, or dreamer you're meant to be.

And seriously, imagine if you didn't wait for the "big" achievement to celebrate. Imagine if you threw yourself a mini party every time you got through a tough writing day. You'd be the happiest writer out there, fueled by your own celebrations and not waiting for the world to notice.

The Power of Self-Love in Your Creative Process

Celebrating yourself isn't just about the grand gestures, though I do highly recommend a dance party in your pajamas every now and then. It's also about the quieter moments—when you give yourself credit for showing up, even when the work doesn't feel Instagram-worthy. It's about recognizing that even on your messiest, least-productive days, you're still making progress.

When you start loving and appreciating yourself for the effort, not just the outcome, something changes. Work becomes less of a slog and more of a joyful process. Each time you show up becomes an act of self-kindness, not just another item to check off your to-do list.

Here's a fun challenge for you: The next time you catch yourself thinking, *"I didn't do enough today,"* flip the script. Instead, say, *"I showed up, and that matters."* When you catch yourself criticizing your progress, remind yourself, *"I'm learning, and that's okay."* Self-love isn't just about bubble baths and indulgences (though those are great). It's about treating yourself with the same compassion you'd show a close friend. Celebrate your effort, even when the results aren't perfect.

Reflect on Your Journey So Far

What have you learned? How have you grown? What challenges have you overcome?

Think back to when you thought about giving up but didn't. Recall when you pushed through the doubt and kept going. Those are your triumphs. Those are the moments that deserve celebration.

Grab your journal and take a few minutes to answer these questions:

- *What is the biggest lesson I've learned on this journey?*
- *What am I most proud of?*
- *How can I celebrate myself today?*

Celebrate that you've come this far—that you've committed to this process and shown up for yourself. This chapter goes beyond marking your progress. It honors your progress.

How to Celebrate You (Yes, You!)

Okay, now for the fun part: *how* do you celebrate yourself? There's no right or wrong answer here, only what feels good to you. Need some ideas? Here's a list to get you started:

- Throw yourself a mini dance party (because who doesn't love dancing to your favorite song in the kitchen?).
- Treat yourself to something indulgent— that fancy coffee with whipped cream or a quiet moment with your favorite book.
- Write a love letter to yourself—tell yourself all the reasons you're proud of how far you've come.
- Give yourself permission to rest. Sometimes, the best way to celebrate is to do absolutely nothing and love every minute of it.
- Share your progress with someone who gets it. Let them hype you up because we all deserve a personal cheer squad.

Whatever you choose, make sure it feels like *you*. Genuinely take a moment to honor your journey and the incredible work you've done.

Moving Forward: Carry Celebration with You

As we move into the next chapter, here's one last thought: don't wait for someone else to validate your progress. Don't wait for a big milestone to celebrate. You are worth celebrating *now*, in this moment, right where you are.

Carry this spirit of celebration with you as you continue your journey. Let it be a reminder that every step—big or small—matters. Your progress is real, and it's worthy of acknowledgment. So, go ahead, keep celebrating yourself every chance you get. After all, *you* are the one doing the work, and you are worth celebrating, always.

We write to taste life twice, in the moment and in retrospect.

— ANAÏS NIN

Outcomes for Chapter 9

By the end of this chapter, you will:

1. Recognize your progress: You'll have learned how to take stock of your journey and appreciate the small victories rather than waiting for one big moment of success.
2. Practice self-love: You'll gain tools to practice self-love and shift your mindset from self-criticism to self-celebration.
3. Build a habit of celebration: You'll learn to consistently celebrate yourself, even for the smallest of accomplishments, creating a positive feedback loop that fuels your creativity and perseverance.

Overall Objective: To balance celebrating your achievements with maintaining forward momentum.

Exercise 1: The Celebration Checklist

Activity: Create a "Celebration Checklist" for the week or month ahead. At the top of the list, write down all the writing goals you'd like to accomplish. Below each goal, leave space to write down how you'll celebrate once you achieve it.

For example:

- Finish Chapter 3 → Treat myself to a fancy latte.
- Write for 5 consecutive days → Go for a scenic walk as a reward.
- Overcome writer's block → Watch my favorite movie guilt-free.

As you accomplish each task, check it off and celebrate as you've planned, even if missed the mark like we mentioned earlier in Chapter 7.

Reflection: How does rewarding yourself after each win feel? Does it motivate you to keep going? This exercise helps you stay focused while still acknowledging your progress.

Exercise 2: Reflect and Project

Objective: To reflect on your achievements while setting new intentions for continued growth.

Activity: Take 15 minutes to write a reflection on your journey so far. List three things you're proud of and how those moments have shaped you as a writer. Then, list three things you'd like to work on moving forward. For each area of improvement, write down one specific step you can take to move toward that goal.

For example:

- I'm proud of overcoming my fear of starting. → Moving forward, I'll aim to write for 30 minutes every morning.
- I'm proud of finishing a short story. → Next, I want to submit it to a contest or share it with my writing group.

Reflection: This exercise allows you to celebrate where you've been while setting your sights on what comes next. How does it feel to balance reflection with forward thinking?

Exercise 3: The Progress Party

Objective: To celebrate your journey with others while continuing to hold yourself accountable.

Activity: Invite a few close friends or fellow writers for a "Progress Party." (This can be in person or virtual.) Each person shares one thing they've accomplished and one thing they're working on moving forward. After each person shares, the group celebrates them—cheers, positive affirmations, or even a dance break!

After the party, write down one piece of advice or encouragement you received that you want to carry with you.

Reflection: How did it feel to share your progress with others? What stood out in their feedback? By making the celebration communal, you'll feel more supported and energized to keep moving forward.

Exercise 4: The Success Playlist

Objective: To create a celebration ritual that keeps you motivated and energized.

Activity: Create a playlist of songs that make you feel like celebrating. These could be upbeat tunes that get you moving or tracks that make you feel empowered. Every time you hit a milestone—big or small—play a song from the playlist and take a moment to dance, sing, or sit back and enjoy the victory.

Reflection: How does having a go-to celebration playlist change how you approach your writing milestones? Does it motivate you to keep reaching new goals?

Final Thoughts

By now, you've done more than write—you've created a reality from your dreams. You're holding something tangible that came from your mind and heart. Whether it's a poem, a memoir, or a novel, you've brought your words to life. This is what Freedom Dreaming is all about—turning what once felt distant and abstract into something real, something impactful. Your next step? Keep manifesting, keep creating, and continue building your legacy.

Chapter 10

Rekindling Your Creative Fire

Reignite your passion for writing and creativity and overcome burnout or creative blocks.

Let's get honest, writing sometimes can break your heart. One moment, you're unstoppable words rushing out like a flood, ideas bursting to life with a kind of magic that makes you believe this is exactly what you were born to do. It's intoxicating, isn't it? But then, just when you're flying high, the words stop. Your mind, once so full of brilliance, hits a wall. Suddenly, the ideas that felt like gold dust evaporate, leaving you staring at the screen in a silent panic. The blank page becomes your adversary, and you wonder—what's a sentence again? Have I reached my own word limit?

Before you start spiraling into self-doubt, imagining your creativity has packed up and left town for good, take a breath. We need to flip this narrative. You're not blocked, and your muse hasn't abandoned you. What you're experiencing is part of the natural ebb and flow of creativity—a tide that retreats only to return even stronger. And right now? We're about to light that fire again.

Like we explored in Chapter 7 with setbacks, writing is a relationship that ebbs and flows. You've already faced moments of doubt and rekindled your creative spirit, but now, let's focus on turning those sparks into sustained passion. It's time to reignite the fire with fresh, fun ways to rediscover your love for words. This chapter goes beyond recognizing the blocks we all face as writers; we did that already. This chapter focuses on reigniting the passion that brought you here in the first place. It may be flickering low, but it hasn't gone out. We're about to stoke those embers and get it burning bright again.

(Spoiler alert: you're not broken. You're just human, and creativity doesn't always appear on demand).

So, instead of panicking when the words don't come easy, let's take a step back, reassess, and reignite that spark. It's time to have some fun with your writing again—no pressure, no expectations, just pure, creative play.

The Rhythm of Creation: Embracing the Lull

Before we leap into strategies, let's address the unsettling quiet that creeps in when creativity seems to vanish. It's not a flaw in your talent or some grand signal of failure. Creativity, like nature itself, moves in cycles. It surges, and it subsides. There are days when the current runs deep, carrying ideas with a force you can barely keep up with. Then, there are days when it retreats, leaving behind only stillness, a vast expanse of silence that feels unnerving.

But the paradox is that stillness is just as vital as the rush. The quiet—the blank page staring back at you—isn't a void; it's fertile ground. It's where seeds take root, where thoughts that haven't yet surfaced start to gestate. Sometimes, it's not about forging forward; it's about stepping back and allowing the deeper currents to stir. Silence, after all, is where whispers gather strength.

This pause is where doubt tries to claw its way in. *Am I still a writer if the words won't come?* you might wonder. Or worse, you begin to question your entire creative purpose. But the lull is part of the symphony. The silence is preparation, not punishment. It's a call to slow down, recalibrate, and nurture what's brewing beneath the surface.

Creativity isn't something to be wrangled into submission. It's a dance, an evolving dialogue between inspiration and effort. And like any meaningful relationship, it thrives on trust, patience, and, yes—sometimes, the playful surrender to what you cannot control. The ebb doesn't take you further from your creative self—it brings you closer to what is yet to be revealed.

Writing doesn't always have to be serious business. When was the last time you *played* with your words? I'm talking about writing just for the heck of it, without worrying about the outcome. The kind of writing where you let yourself go a little wild, a little weird, and maybe even a little ridiculous.

Here's how we're going to reignite that creative fire:

1. **Change Your Scenery** - Sick of the same desk? Go write in a coffee shop, a park, or even your car (parked, of course). Switching up your environment can spark new ideas.

2. **Genre Hopping** - If you've been stuck in one genre, why not dip your toes into something completely different? Write a horror story if you usually write romance. Or blend genres—like a sci-fi Western with a side of poetry. The weirder, the better!

3. **Doodle Your Ideas** - When words won't come, let your hand doodle across the page. Draw your characters, scribble random ideas, or map out scenes with stick figures. Sometimes, your brain needs to switch gears before the words flow.

4. **Write Something Terrible** - Seriously, permit yourself to write something lousy—just for fun. Write the worst, most cliché-filled dialogue you can think of. It's like stretching your muscles before a run. Once the pressure's off, the real magic starts.

Fall Back in Love with Writing

It's so easy to lose ourselves in the relentless pursuit of deadlines, the grip of perfectionism, and the constant pressure to churn out polished work. These demands are undeniably part of the writing journey, but they can also suffocate the very thing that brought us here in the first place—the joy. When the weight of expectations becomes too heavy, it can drain the magic right out of the creative process, turning something once liberating into a burden.

But creativity was never meant to be a grind—it's meant to be a wild, unrestrained flow of joy, a space where freedom and self-expression thrive without boundaries.

So, let's make a pact - From now on, let's focus on enjoying the process. Let's chase that feeling of creative freedom that first sparked your love for writing. And remember what Ernest Hemingway said: *"The first draft of anything is shit."* So why stress about it? Write with abandon, have some fun, and let the editing come later. The world needs your voice, run-on sentences and all.

Show up, show up,
show up, and after a while
the muse shows up too.

– ISABEL ALLENDE

Outcomes for Chapter 10

By the end of this chapter, you will:

1. Reignite Passion: You'll rediscover the joy of writing by focusing on fun, play, and creativity rather than perfection or outcomes.
2. Break the Routine: You'll break out of stale writing habits and environments, injecting new energy and excitement into your work.
3. Overcome Creative Blocks: By exploring playful strategies, you'll develop tools to overcome creative fatigue, self-doubt, and perfectionism.
4. Strengthen Your Writing Practice: You'll learn how to sustain your creative fire by allowing room for exploration, play, and experimentation in your writing life.
5. Reclaim Your Voice: By embracing the untidy, imperfect writing process, you'll reconnect with your authentic voice and remember why you started writing in the first place.

Overall Objective: This chapter helps bring back the fun and reignite your creative fire. Below are some innovative and playful exercises designed to help you shake things up, rediscover the joy of writing, and get those creative juices flowing again. Remember, the key here is to play—to explore without the pressure of perfection and have fun with the process.

Exercise 1: The "Weird Place, Weird Idea" Writing Challenge

Objective: To break out of routine and spark creativity by writing in an unusual place or from an unusual perspective.

Activity: Pick a place where you've never written before. Maybe it's under a tree, on your stoop, or even in the bathtub (be careful with that one!). Once you're settled, challenge yourself to write something totally off-the-wall. Maybe it's a story from the perspective of an inanimate object—a spoon, a traffic light, or your left shoe. Don't think too hard; just go with the first bizarre idea that pops into your head.

Reflection: How did writing in a new location or from a strange perspective shake up your creative process? Did you feel more free to explore different ideas? Use this as a reminder that sometimes all you need is a change of scenery or mindset to reignite your spark.

Exercise 2: Genre Swap Speed-Writing

Objective: To challenge your brain by writing in a genre that's completely outside your comfort zone.

Activity: Set a timer for 15 minutes. Pick a genre you never write in—fantasy, mystery, romance, horror, whatever feels the most foreign to you. Now, speed-write a scene or a mini-story in that genre. No editing, no second-guessing. Just let your imagination run wild and see what comes out.

Reflection: Did writing in a different genre give you new ideas or a fresh perspective? Sometimes, leaping into unfamiliar territory is all it takes to get your creativity flowing again. Plus, it's fun to shake things up!

Exercise 3: The Nostalgia Dive

Objective: To rekindle your passion by tapping into the books, movies, or music that first made you fall in love with storytelling.

Activity: Think back to when you first discovered your love for writing. Was there a book, movie, or song that sparked your imagination? Revisit it now. Re-read your favorite chapter, re-watch that film, or play that song on repeat. Then, write a short piece inspired by that old favorite—maybe it's a reflection, a poem, or a new story idea it brings to mind.

Reflection: Did revisiting an old favorite stir up memories of why you started writing in the first place? Let that nostalgic spark remind you that the passion is still there, just waiting to be rekindled.

Exercise 4: The "What If?" Game

Objective: To reignite curiosity and creativity by exploring wild possibilities.

Activity: Write a list of "What if?" questions related to your current project, or just for fun. For example:

- What if my protagonist had a secret superpower they didn't know about?
- What if this story took place on a different planet?
- What if the villain is the hero's long-lost sibling?

Pick one "What if?" question and write a quick scene based on it. Let yourself go down the rabbit hole of possibilities.

Reflection: Did this exercise give you any new ideas or directions to explore? Sometimes, asking "What if?" opens up new creative paths you hadn't considered.

These exercises are designed to reintroduce playfulness and curiosity into your writing routine. By shaking up your process, experimenting with new approaches, and centering joy, you'll reignite the passion that makes writing such a fulfilling creative outlet. Let these exercises serve as a reminder that writing is about exploring, playing, and creating.

Final Thoughts

You've reignited the fire within and overcome the blocks that held you back. The passion you felt when you first started writing has returned, stronger than ever. Keep this energy alive as you move forward, knowing that you can push through any obstacle that comes your way.

Chapter 11

From Dream to Reality

Translate your dreams and aspirations into tangible written work.

In Chapter 8, when we talked about authenticity, you unlocked the power of your unique voice, and in Chapter 9, you celebrated the small wins that brought you here. Now, we're taking that voice and all your triumphs and channeling them into something tangible—something real that will carry your Freedom Dream forward. We're on to the next big adventure. It's time to transform those beautiful words into something tangible. Something you can hold, share, and—let's be honest—brag about just a little bit.

Now I get it. Your goal might not be to publish, but that's okay. If writing is your form of personal freedom, a way to express and liberate yourself, that's more than enough. This chapter isn't here to shove you into the world of "publish or perish," especially if you're not feeling it. But stick with me because even if you don't plan to publish, there may be some nuggets in here you can pass along to a friend, a student, or that one family member who's been talking about writing a book for years.

And remember, when you're feeling liberated, you naturally want to share that light. It's like when Bath & Body Works has a ridiculous candle sale.

You've got enough candles to light up Times Square, but you still text your bestie, "GO NOW—sale ends at midnight!" You're feeling good, and you want to share the wealth. That's the same energy we're bringing here.

Whether you decide to publish or not, know this: I see you as a **NEW YORK TIMES BESTSELLER** in the making. That's *my* Freedom Dream for you, and trust me, it's manifesting.

So, what's the next step?

Let's jump into the exciting, practical, and slightly terrifying process of turning those ideas into a full-blown masterpiece. Whether you're writing poetry, a novel, a memoir, or something that defies genre, this chapter will guide you through what it takes to bring your creation to life.

Ready to turn those dreams into something tangible? Let's go!

From Inspiration to Publication: Making It Happen

We've all had those, *aha!* Moments—when inspiration strikes, leaving you with a story or idea that won't let go. But how do you turn that spark of brilliance into a polished, publishable piece of art that resonates with others?

1. Purpose Over Perfection

Let's set this straight right from the start: not every word you write needs to be perfect, but it does need a purpose. Before diving into your masterpiece, take a moment to ask yourself, *Why am I writing this?* Simon Sinek famously said, "Start with why," and it's a powerful place to begin. Do you want to inspire, challenge, or entertain? Having a clear purpose will give your writing direction and keep you grounded when self-doubt creeps in (because it will, but you know how to deal with it). Your purpose is your compass, reminding you why your story matters and why the world needs to hear it.

2. Crafting the Structure

Now that you've defined your purpose, let's build the bones of your piece. Structure is like the skeleton of your story—without it, things can get a little floppy. Take some time to create an outline. What's the main message or theme you want to convey? How will you build tension? How will you wrap it all up? A roadmap (even a loose one) will keep your writing focused and prevent those "Wait, what was I even trying to say?" moments.

3. Embrace the Magic of Editing

Your first draft is supposed is a brain dump of all your ideas. But editing is where you polish that raw brilliance into something cohesive, sharp, and powerful. Revisit your work, trim the fat, and clarify your message. It's like gardening—sometimes, you've got to prune away the excess to let the best parts shine through.

4. The Power of Feedback

Before you send your work out into the world, let it marinate with a trusted circle. Share it with a friend, a writer's group, or professional editor. Feedback is essential. It's like getting a sneak peek into how your readers will experience your work. Listen to what resonates and what falls flat, and use that insight to make your piece even stronger. Constructive criticism isn't an attack—it's a tool to help elevate your writing.

Understanding Your Publishing Options

Let's talk about getting your work *out there*. The beauty of being a writer today is that there are more publishing options than ever before. Whether you're drawn to traditional publishing or self-publishing, there's a path for you.

1. Traditional Publishing

If you're looking for the full package—editorial support, marketing, distribution—traditional publishing might be your route. This means working with a literary agent to get your book into the hands of a publishing house. But keep in mind, it's a competitive game. Expect rejection (seriously, it's part of the process), but stay persistent.

Action Step: Start by researching literary agents in your genre and craft a killer query letter. This letter should be short, snappy, and showcase why your work deserves their attention. Your story is unique—make sure they know it.

2. Self-Publishing

Want to maintain creative control and get your work into the world faster? Self-publishing gives you that freedom. But with freedom comes responsibility. You'll need to oversee everything from editing to cover design to marketing. It's a lot, but if you're a DIY kind of person, it can be incredibly rewarding.

Action Step: If you go this route, hire a professional editor and cover designer. You want your book to stand out, which means making sure it looks and reads like something you'd pick up in a bookstore.

3. Digital Platforms & Blogs

Not ready to commit to a full-blown book? No worries. Platforms like Medium, Wattpad, or even a personal blog are fantastic ways to get your writing out there, build an audience, and get feedback before diving into something bigger. Think of it as testing the waters before you cannonball into the publishing world.

Rejection: A Step Closer to Success

Let's face it: rejection is part of the writing journey. Even the greats—Rowling, King, Angelou—faced a mountain of rejection slips before they got their break. It's not a reflection of your talent; it's just the nature of the game.

Action Step: When you face rejection (because it's *when*, not *if*), don't take it personally. Refine your work, tweak your pitch, and send it out again. Persistence is the key that unlocks doors.

Manifest Your Published Reality

Here's the big takeaway: whether your dream is to see your name on a bookshelf, to share your words online, or to pass your work along to a small circle of friends, you're turning your *Freedom Dream* into a tangible reality. You're no longer *just writing*—you are an AUTHOR!

And let's not forget: this entire process is part of the Freedom Dreaming we've been practicing from the start. You're manifesting something real from the depths of your imagination. This is what it's all about: bringing your dreams into the light, one word at a time.

Many stories matter. Stories have been used to dispossess and to malign. But stories can also be used to empower, and to humanize. Stories can break the dignity of a people. But stories can also repair that broken dignity.

— CHIMAMANDA NGOZI ADICHIE

Outcomes for Chapter 11

By the end of this chapter, you will:

1. Solidify why you're writing and how your message serves your creative goals.
2. Better understand how to build your story's structure and keep it focused.
3. Embrace editing as the process that polishes your work and sharpens your message.
4. Learn to give and receive constructive feedback that elevates your writing.
5. Explore various publishing routes and identify the one that suits your goals.
6. Be equipped to handle rejection as a pathway, not a dead end, in your writing journey.

Overall Objective: This chapter empowers you to clarify your intent, visualize success, and navigate rejection with strength. You'll also explore different publishing paths, breaking the process into manageable steps and guiding you from dream to reality of becoming a published author.

Exercise 1: Purpose Over Perfection

Objective: Clarify the intention behind your writing and use it as a guide when self-doubt strikes.

Activity: Write down the purpose behind your current project. Why are you writing this? Is it to inspire? To provoke thought? To entertain?

Break this down into three actionable statements:

- "I'm writing this because __________."
- "My readers will take away __________."
- "This story matters because __________."

Reflection: Keep these answers near your writing space to remind yourself why your voice matters. When you face self-doubt, revisit these statements to refocus and push forward.

Exercise 2: The Candle Method – Lighting Your Way Forward

Objective: To symbolically "light the way" through any doubts or procrastination that may hold you back.

Instructions:

- Light a candle (preferably one that holds personal significance or an uplifting scent). Sit quietly for a few moments and focus on the flame.
- As the candle burns, visualize it lighting the path of your writing journey. See it illuminating each stage, from rough drafts to published work.
- After this brief visualization, spend 15 minutes freewriting about the barriers you've faced in your writing and how you'll overcome them. Imagine the candlelight burning away any doubts or fears.
- Blow out the candle as a symbolic act of closing this chapter of hesitation and gliding fully into your writing future.

Exercise 3: The Power of Feedback

Objective: Gain valuable insights and improve your work by seeking external perspectives.

Activity: Choose one piece of writing you're ready to share. Identify 2-3 trusted people (friends, writing group members, editors) to provide feedback.

- Ask them to highlight what worked, what resonated, and what didn't land as intended.
- Give them 1-2 specific areas you'd like advice on (e.g., character development, pacing).

Reflection: After receiving feedback, write down the most helpful takeaways. Reflect on what surprised you and how you plan to implement the suggestions. Remember: feedback is a tool for growth, but you don't have to incorporate every piece of advice.

Exercise 4: Manifestation Writing – Write Your Future Review

Objective: To help the writer visualize success and create a positive affirmation of their work.

Instructions:

- Imagine your book has been published and is out in the world. Now, write a review of your work from the perspective of a future reader or critic. What praise is being given? How does your work stand out? What emotions are readers experiencing?
- Be as specific and as detailed as possible. What quotes or passages are people talking about? How has your book touched or inspired them?

This exercise helps you tap into the feeling of success and accomplishment, solidifying your vision of bringing your project to life.

Exercise 5: Bouncing Back from Rejection

Objective: Normalize rejection as part of the creative process and learn how to grow from it.

Activity:

- Write down a list of 3 famous authors or creators who faced rejection before they succeeded.
- Next, write about a time you faced rejection (writing or otherwise) and reflect on how it impacted you.
- Now, rewrite that narrative. How can you view that rejection as a catalyst rather than a setback?

Reflection: Commit to seeing future rejections as part of the process. Keep the names of those who persisted despite failure as a reminder that you're in good company.

Exercise 6: Building Your Publishing Dream

Objective: Explore different publishing options and start planning for your path forward.

Activity: Research one publishing route that interests you (traditional, self-publishing, digital).

- List the required steps (query letters, marketing, design, etc.).
- Break the process into manageable tasks. What's the first step you can take this week? Reflection: Choose the publishing route that aligns best with your goals, lifestyle, and creative freedom. What excites you most about this journey? What challenges are you ready to face head-on?

Final Thoughts

You've transformed your dreams into something tangible, taking the brave step to bring your words into the world. Whether you've decided to publish or share your work with those closest to you, you've made your dream tangible. This is the culmination of all your hard work, a true manifestation of your Freedom Dream. The world is ready for your voice—now let it be heard.

Chapter 12

Your Story, Your Legacy

Embrace writing as a lifelong journey, continuously evolving and growing as a writer and individual.

Dear Author (because that's *exactly* who you are now!),

Look at you. Seriously, *look* at you. You've made it through this entire journey, and here we are at the final chapter of this journal. Take a second to soak that in. Breathe deeply, let it out slowly, and reflect on how far you've come. Remember when you first cracked open this journal, maybe a little nervous, perhaps a little excited, unsure of where it would take you? And now? You've made it through introspection, storytelling, digging deep into your identity, facing procrastination like a boss, and fine-tuning your beautiful, unique voice.

I am SO proud of you. Truly. It's been an honor walking this road with you. I'm officially your friend in your head now. Oh yeah, we've been through it all together! We've cried, spilled coffee, comforted our fears, gotten vulnerable, shared a drink (or two), laughed until we couldn't breathe, and even danced a little. Admit it, we're friends now. There's no going back.

Let's talk about the next phase of the adventure, and no, this isn't the "end." In fact, it's more like a beginning. You've spent time pouring your heart into these pages, discovering what *Freedom Dreaming* means for you—turning your dreams into reality, word by word, breath by breath. You've taken your ideas and made them tangible.

You're not done yet. Not even close.

Your Journal: The Ultimate Sidekick

Before we wrap up, let's give a little love to something that's been with you through this entire journey: your journal. I told you from the start that this isn't just an ordinary book. It's been your sidekick, your confidante, and where your most profound thoughts have found a home. Together, you've scribbled down dreams, uncovered fears, and navigated the messiness of being human.

But guess what? Your journal still has so much potential. YOU still have so much potential.

What Comes Next?

As you continue writing, remember a few things:

1. Consistency Is Your Best Friend

Even if it's just five minutes a day, keep showing up. Writing is a relationship; like all good relationships, it thrives on consistency. Some days will be easy; others might feel like wading through mud, but every word counts.

2. Look Back and Reflect

From time to time, flip back through these pages. You'll be amazed at how much you've grown and how far your thoughts have traveled. Reflection is a powerful tool—it allows you to see where you've been and where you're heading.

3. Set Challenges, Just for Fun

Get playful with your creativity. Set mini-challenges for yourself—write about something you've never explored before, or tackle a completely random prompt. Make it fun! Who knows? You might surprise yourself with where your words take you.

4. Share Your Words

When you're ready, share what you've written. Whether with a close friend, a fellow writer, or even the world, it's an incredible feeling to let your words out into the open. And trust me, someone out there needs to hear what you have to say.

5. Celebrate Everything

Yes, every. Single. Thing. You finished a page? Celebrate! You wrote a line that made you tear up or laugh out loud? Celebrate! Acknowledging these small wins will keep you motivated and remind you of the joy in this process. Treat yourself, throw a solo dance party, or take a moment to smile and recognize your brilliance.

Freedom Dreaming in Action

Now, let's not forget what brought us here in the first place—*Freedom Dreaming*. You've been doing it all along! Each chapter and sentence has been you actively manifesting the life and creative journey you've been dreaming of. Your dreams are no longer just floating in your head; they're becoming real with every page you fill and every risk you take.

You're creating your future, one word at a time.

Hold fast to dreams, for if dreams die, life is a broken-winged bird that cannot fly.

— LANGSTON HUGHES

Outcomes for Chapter 12

By the end of this chapter, you will:

- Reflect on and celebrate your journey—every word, struggle, and triumph.
- Remember the power of daily writing and understand that showing up regularly is vital to growth.
- Embrace the idea of playful experimentation, setting challenges to keep your creativity fresh and thriving.
- Value the act of looking back at your progress to motivate and guide your future writing.
- Make a habit of celebrating every win, big or small, and remember that the process itself is worth honoring.
- Realize your freedom dreams and acknowledge that they aren't just dreams anymore—they're becoming your lived reality through the act of writing.

Overall Objective: These exercises invite you to reflect on your personal transformation throughout this journal while also setting a clear vision for your ongoing creative journey. You'll identify critical breakthroughs through guided prompts, explore your liberation story, and commit to the path ahead with clarity and intention.

Exercise 1: Growth Timeline

1. List each chapter title from this journal.

▸ For each chapter, jot down the title on the left side of your page.

2. Identify a revelation or breakthrough for each chapter.

▸ Next to each chapter, write a sentence or two highlighting one major insight or moment of growth you experienced in that chapter. It could be anything from discovering your unique voice to overcoming procrastination. Think of these as key markers on your journey.

3. Reflect on your transformation.

▸ Look at your timeline. What patterns do you notice? Can you see the trajectory of your growth? Does a common theme emerge? This exercise is all about seeing how far you've come and appreciating the work you've done to get here.

Exercise 2: Invitation to the Liberation Gala – My Journey to Empower Yours

In this exercise, you'll revisit your Liberation Gala essay from earlier in the journal, but with a twist: now, you're in charge of planning the event and inviting others. This one is called the Freedom Gala. You're no longer just attending—you're hosting.

1. Write the invitation.

- ▸ Open with an invitation to your readers, offering them a seat at your Freedom Gala. Describe the theme: freedom, joy, and the beauty of the journey.

2. Share your personal liberation story.

- ▸ This is where you get real. Share the highs and lows of your writing journey. What struggles did you overcome? What truths did you discover about yourself? Let others know that liberation doesn't happen in a straight line—it's a dance between breakthroughs and setbacks.

3. Center joy.

- ▸ How have you learned to center joy in your journey? Let them know that while the road may be challenging, joy keeps us moving. Leave them with a warm, encouraging note, letting them know they're capable of their transformation, too.

4. Speak to what this Freedom feels like.

- ▸ Describe the feeling you are having in that moment—what it feels like to shed old fears, expectations, and self-doubt. Paint a picture of how liberation looks and feels now that you've moved through the process. Is it lighter? More empowering? Share the joy of no longer carrying the those naggin limitations, and invite your guests to imagine that for themselves.

5. Offer encouragement and wisdom.

▶ Think about the insights you've gained through this process. How can they benefit others? Speak from a place of wisdom, inviting your guests (readers) to join you on the journey toward self-expression and liberation.

Exercise 3: Commitment Pledge

Crafting a personal commitment pledge solidifies your intention to continue this journey—no matter what challenges arise.

1. Draft your pledge.

▶ Write a personal commitment to yourself. What promises will you make to keep writing, dreaming, and pushing past creative blocks? Maybe it's a promise never to let procrastination stop you again or a vow to trust your unique voice even when doubt creeps in.

2. Sign your pledge.

▶ Once you've written your commitment, sign it. Print it out if you're writing digitally, or write it by hand. Keep this pledge near your writing space as a visual reminder of the promises you've made to yourself.

3. Revisit as needed.

▶ When motivation wanes (because it will, and that's okay), return to this pledge. Let it remind you why you started this journey in the first place.

Exercise 4: The Next Chapter

Our book may have 12 chapters, but your story doesn't stop here. Imagine what Chapter 13 of your life and writing journey might look like.

1. Imagine the next chapter.

- If you were to write Chapter 13 of your journey, what would it entail? Would it be a chapter of creative expansion filled with new projects or a deeper dive into a specific theme or genre?

2. Identify challenges, goals, and hopes.

- Write down the challenges you anticipate facing in this next phase. Maybe it's balancing writing with life commitments or learning to market your work.
- Next, set some goals. What do you hope to achieve creatively, personally, or professionally?
- Finally, jot down your hopes for this next chapter. What kind of growth do you see for yourself? How do you hope your writing will continue to evolve?

Final Thoughts

You've reached the end of this journal, but this is just the beginning of your journey. Look at the milestones you've hit: you've discovered your true self, empowered your voice, confronted your barriers, taken action, and manifested your dreams. But the most beautiful part of this process is that it never stops. There are always more stories to tell, more dreams to chase, and more layers of yourself to discover. Keep writing, keep dreaming, and remember: your journey is yours to create, one word at a time.

Congratulations and Farewell

(for now)

We've reached the end of our journey together **Congratulations!** What you've accomplished here is extraordinary. You've poured your heart, soul, and energy into this process, which takes courage. You've been on a liberatory path that is bigger than just words. It is one of self-discovery, of peeling back doubts and transforming them into dreams. You've turned those dreams into something real and lasting.

When I began this journal, I was in a place where I felt silenced and dismissed. I had let someone take my voice and dim my passion, and it left me questioning everything about myself. But eventually, I sat with that pain. I let it burn until it became the fuel for creating something meaningful. Now, I'm passing that torch to you. This is the circle of growth—we rise, and as we do, we lift others with us.

You began this journey seeking liberation, the process of freeing yourself from the layers that once held you back. And now? You're standing fully in your **freedom**. The quest for liberation got you here, but freedom is what you've claimed. And let me tell you, I am so confident in you. I have no doubt you've unlocked a powerful version of yourself, one ready to move through the world boldly and unapologetically. And I can almost see it—you're smiling right now. That knowing, radiant smile of someone who has embraced their freedom.

You aren't the only person feeling this transformation. It is rippling out to everyone around you. You've tapped into a movement that will inspire others just by being fully yourself. If I could choose the perfect soundtrack to capture this moment, it would be **Earth, Wind & Fire's "September"**—a celebration of joy, life, and the moments that have brought you to this place. You've arrived. You're here. **Freedom**.

I See You, I Appreciate You

Here's something I want you to remember: the world has been waiting for your voice. It's more complete because you are here, sharing your truth. You've connected yourself to a legacy, walking alongside those who came before you and setting a foundation for those who will follow. You stand shoulder to shoulder with literary giants and your ancestors. Your voice matters, and it is a gift that we are privileged to receive.

As you step into this next chapter of your life, remember that the world of words is vast and beautiful, just like your journey. Every story and idea that flows from your heart is another piece of the legacy you are building. And let me tell you, your story is far from over—this is just the beginning. What you've written here has been magnificent, but there is so much more waiting to be born from the depths of your soul.

Thank you for trusting me and this journal to walk beside you on this extraordinary path. And thank you for sharing your heart, your dreams, and your journey. Here's to the many more pages that will soon be filled with (insert your name here) ____________________________ words. The world is listening and eager to hear what you have to say.

With the deepest admiration, pride, and anticipation,

Nicole Yarde

About the Author

Nicole Yarde merges education, social justice, and artistic passion, championing community upliftment and empowerment. Throughout her 20-year career in education, she has consistently focused on enhancing the lives of students, educators, and families, especially within historically neglected communities. Her initiatives are deeply rooted in humanity, social justice, and holistic well-being, ensuring that everyone, regardless of their background, is approached with a lens of equity, allowing them to thrive and grow.

Throughout her career, she has been a staunch advocate for progressive programs. From promoting social-emotional learning to advancing liberatory education, Nicole has consistently pushed the boundaries, introducing innovative approaches that educate, empower, and inspire every individual she engages with. Her vision goes beyond conventional education; she dreams and delivers an education that sees, hears, and responds to every individual, ensuring a space where all feel valued and understood.

But beyond the titles, Nicole finds solace in writing, a medium through which she encourages and inspires countless others to chase after their dreams. ut beyond the titles, Nicole finds solace in writing, a medium through which she encourages and inspires countless others to chase after their dreams. She has also created the platform Black Rewrite www.blackrewrite.com. Black Rewrite is an initiative focused on amplifying and celebrating the narratives of Black and Brown authors. It operates as a platform dedicated to combatting the systematic erasure of these voices from the literary world. Black Rewrite recognizes the importance of diverse storytelling and the rich experiences that Black and Brown authors bring to literature. When she's not championing educational programs or penning her thoughts, Nicole immerses herself in movies, travels the globe with a special love for her native home, Barbados, or experiments with new recipes, adding her unique Caribbean touch.

In *Not Just Words: Writing as Liberation*, Nicole encapsulates her love for writing and her belief in the transformative power of self-expression. Through this work, she hopes to inspire the path for many others, guiding them toward their own journeys of self-discovery, liberation, and realization of dreams.

Nicole holds a Bachelor of Arts in Journalism and English from CUNY and a Masters in International Education from NYU and lives in Brooklyn.

Want to share your thoughts? The author would love to hear from you. Reach out at info@blackrewrite.com

Follow me on Instagram @angie_ed or @black_rewrite

Visit: www.nicoleyarde.com